CLIMBING INTO MY DREAM

An Aerospace Engineer's Journey

WILLIAM DYE

iUniverse, Inc.
Bloomington

Climbing into My Dream
An Aerospace Engineer's Journey

iUniverse books may be ordered through booksellers or by contacting:

iUniverse
1663 Liberty Drive
Bloomington, IN 47403
www.iuniverse.com
1-800-Authors (1-800-288-4677)

ISBN: 978-1-4620-2388-2 (sc)
ISBN: 978-1-4620-2389-9 (hc)
ISBN: 978-1-4620-2390-5 (ebk)

Printed in the United States of America

iUniverse rev. date: 10/14/2011

Dedication

To my mother, for supporting and sharing my childhood
dream; and to my father for guiding me toward it.
To my wife, Joyce, for her never-ending support
throughout my aerospace career.

Acknowledgments

I would like to thank my wife, Joyce, for her constant support and encouragement as I worked through the long process of writing this memoir. Thanks, also, to my sister, Patty Young, who many times said, "Keep going" when I was discouraged. And warm thanks to my editor, Susan Snowden, who helped me "tighten" my rambling early drafts and become a more efficient storyteller.

Contents

FOREWORD

Bill Dye's journey has been one that captures a unique personal experience through "space and time" as our nation's venture into space unfolded and matured. While there are thousands of aerospace engineers who have engaged in our line of business, few have been "into space," so colorful, and as remarkably productive as Bill. As one who has been in the business, and now retired after forty-two years, I can say with certainty that Bill is one of the "unique" and "high valued" colleagues I had the pleasure to know and work with.

Bill's final chapter about working with us on Space Imaging and IKONOS is truly the kind of gratifying "book end" to an exciting career we all seek to have. His "dream" was realized the moment that first high-resolution digital image came down from "his" satellite, IKONOS, 438 miles above us, moving overhead at four miles per second.

In our line of business there are very few "aha moments" when you know and feel the personal satisfaction of unquestioned excellence in what you have just done. But in this case what was done went far beyond the norms of most of our national and commercial space ventures. He/we indeed changed the way we see ourselves, and in so doing changed history forever.

So, two relevant thoughts about Bill and his career from two exceptional individuals, one I knew and one I didn't: Sir Arthur Clarke and Socrates. For Clarke, IKONOS gave rise to the "Dawn of the Age of Transparency," and even he was in awe of our commercial accomplishment. I met with him in Sri Lanka in early 2004 shortly after the severe tsunami struck his country and the region. When one receives acknowledgment from such a prophet of space ventures, it is clear that we and Bill's team accomplished something very unique and very important. Clarke was mesmerized by how the image of Sri Lanka was taken with such clarity and precision from so far away. That comment from Clarke evokes the memory of his own "Second Law": "Any sufficiently advanced technology is indistinguishable from magic." For Sir Arthur Clarke, IKONOS was a magical thing. Bill's "dream" turned into magic.

...and then there was Socrates, a few millennia prior, who was quoted to have said: "Man must rise above the Earth, to the top of the clouds and beyond, for only thus will he fully understand the world in which he lives." For someone who holds a dream as deeply as Bill did for so many years and through so many challenges, this reward to have changed the world is more than can be asked or expected of one. For Bill, space was not about a job but rather a journey through life to have that euphoric moment when you indeed reached for the stars and grabbed them to let us all look down upon our world and work to make it a better place for all.

I would encourage all those in pursuit of their "dream," whether to venture into space, science, art, literature, medicine, etc., to let their dream inwardly motivate them and never wander far from the path to that "aha moment."

John Neer

Founder and First CEO, Space Imaging Co.
Vice President, Lockheed Martin Space Systems Company (retired)

Introduction

Throughout my career many people have asked me, "So what is it like, really, working in aerospace?" And, "How did you get interested in aerospace, anyway?" This collection of stories will provide answers to each of those questions. It will also shed some light on why others within aerospace corporations, NASA, the government, the military, or the myriad of subcontractors and suppliers of aerospace equipment sought out the romance of flight and the excitement of space travel.

This is my view of aerospace from literally cradle to, hopefully not anytime soon, grave. I share my childhood experiences, dreams, interests, and motivations to show how they led to my professional life's path. As with most people and just about any career there were times of excitement, anxiety, disillusionment, and gratification at just about every stage. There were many times I asked myself if the stress and the frustrations were all worth it. The answer was usually yes. There were exceptions and certainly toward the end of my career the frustration began to outweigh the excitement.

What made the journey well worth the effort were the people I worked with and the missions we accomplished. I feel that I contributed by applying common sense and "sanity" where it was sometimes lacking. Hopefully the early stories will illustrate how common sense and "keep it simple" should be fostered today in young engineers, and young people in general.

I enjoyed very much mentoring the younger engineers. Admittedly it makes one feel important but, honestly, I genuinely enjoyed "giving back" and sharing my triumphs and especially my mistakes, whether technical or political, with them. Sometimes they looked at me in amazement after I told them about some risky or "crude but it got the job done" thing we did years before which, at the time, wasn't a big deal. I remember that amazed look on their faces. I had that look; we all had it back then when we looked into our dinosaur elders' eyes and listened to *their* stories, hanging on every word, and hoping *our* future experiences would be even half the fun they described. They were.

Throughout my life and career, I never really took myself seriously. My work I took seriously but I believed in having fun with everything; otherwise, what's the point? Quite often I'd say, "If you're not laughing, you're dead."

Unlike other books on aerospace written by ex-CEOs or other high ranking aerospace executives, this one will be a tad more from "in the trenches." I did make it to middle management and I am completely satisfied with the level I achieved. These stories don't focus on the business side of the industry, but rather on some of the more amusing situations I experienced throughout my career, things that just might paint a truer picture of what working in aerospace was like.

As you will see, I enjoy telling stories and I'm sure this collection will give you some insight into what made me choose aerospace, the path to get there, what it was like being there and, frankly, why it's now great to be done with it all.

It Started with a Dream

I

All of my childhood memories are vivid. I can remember the crib—honest. One of my earliest memories is of looking up from the baby stroller at airplanes flying over our little bungalow outside of Pittsburgh, Pennsylvania. My parents realized right off the bat that I loved airplanes. They took me to the Allegheny Airport many times so I could watch these magnificent machines for as long as they could stand it, which was never long enough for me.

I was born in August 1949, and when I was only three or four years old I drew sketches of airplanes and could recognize their different features. I particularly remember seeing DC-3s and DC-6s flying over. Of course, all I saw were the distinctive features of each type of airplane, like the wing shape of the DC-3 and its two engines and how it varied from the four-engine airliner, the DC-6. The names and designations would come later.

My grandfather, Roy Dye Sr., had given my parents a drawing table, a unique table with a tilt-able surface and constructed so its support base would slide under a bed or chair. I drew pictures of airplanes on this table. But I didn't want to draw just a side view of an airplane. No, I wanted to draw it as if I were looking at it in the flesh; I wanted to draw it in 3-D. So I drew a circle and then some slanted lines for the top and bottom of the fuselage. But when I tried to draw the wings, they just didn't look right. At this early age I couldn't grasp the "perspective" thing. There was something missing. I couldn't figure it out, and I can still remember the frustration. This was my rather inauspicious start on the road that would be my life's work, the pursuit of capturing the essence of machines, of things that moved, especially flying machines.

Author drawing airplanes; 1953

* * *

I was born cross-eyed. This feature, unless corrected, would have made for an even *more* interesting school life. I donned "occluders" (strips of tape covering just the inside portion of my field of vision to help correct my eyes), which didn't work, and pairs of little eyeglasses, which I destroyed every other week.

I went through all kinds of eye surgery in an attempt to correct my crossed eyes, and wore eye patches after those operations when I was only two years old. But the surgeries weren't entirely successful, so Mother took me to the Pittsburgh Children's Hospital many times for eye exercises. "Now watch the red clothespin," the nurse would say as she moved this low-tech item back and forth, back and forth. These didn't work either.

My eyes would be the biggest challenge of my life, greatly impacting my self-esteem and assertiveness while I was growing up, as well as dramatically changing the course of my professional goals.

I think I remember those trips to Pittsburgh so clearly because they were an adventure. To get to Pittsburgh Mother put me in a little red wagon and pulled me to a bus stop a few blocks from our house on Robin Drive in Foxcroft, a neighborhood near Mt. Lebanon that was just on the other side of the Liberty tubes (tunnels) to Pittsburgh. She parked the wagon behind the bus stop that was at the bottom of a street in a wooded area. The bus took us right to the heart of downtown Pittsburgh, to the Jenkins Arcade. From there we took a trolley car up Forbes Avenue to the hospital, the eye doctor, or both. When we came home later that evening, the red wagon was still there. And it was there every time.

I remembered her determination, her cleverness, and her ability to "just do it" or "just get it done any way you can and with what you've got." This was a rather large brick in my foundation—learning to think of alternatives and to find that little red wagon on every project.

My mother, Anne, said she was half Swiss and half German but years later I found out we were mostly Swiss and Polish with a tad German. She was small and was renowned for her humor and wit. She suffered constantly from severe migraine headaches. Later we would accompany her to doctors, specialists, and even hypnotherapists. Throughout my childhood I would see her suffering in bed for days at a time, yet she would drag herself out of bed to make dinner. Partially because she felt it was her job, but she also she had a touch of the martyr. Of course, my dad couldn't or wouldn't even think of making his own dinner; but to be fair, he, my sister Patty, and I had stewed tomatoes for dinner a number of times. Unfortunately, I inherited the migraine gene but, fortunately, my headaches were not nearly as severe as hers.

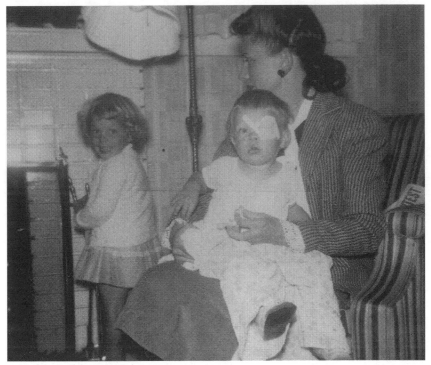

Author, mother and sister Patty; 1950

2

About two weeks before my sixth birthday, I got a letter in the mail. A letter! Me! I was five years and 351 days old. I noticed that it was a fat letter, a lumpy letter. Who gets lumpy letters? Mother opened it. Inside there was a note with one piece of Bazooka Joe Bubble Gum taped to it. Mom read the note—although I was never allowed to call her Mom; it had to be Mother. But, hey, in my mind I could call her anything, and in my teens there were other things in my mind too that I wanted to call her. I can't remember precisely what the note said but it was something like:

Dear Billy Dye,

Hi, my name is Kent. I hear you will be my new neighbor.

I'd like to be your friend.

Kent Sargent

A fan! A letter to me. Did my terrific, outgoing, almost six-year-old personality and reputation precede me? But wait. What's this about moving?

A few weeks later, on my birthday, we moved. My dad, Peter Hamilton Dye, worked at the Jones & Laughlin Steel Corporation in personnel and labor relations. They transferred him from the J&L Pittsburgh works to the J&L works at Aliquippa, a small steel mill town of about twenty-five thousand people, seventeen miles down the Ohio River from Pittsburgh. But, at the time, I had no idea where we were going. The moving van came and I climbed all over the truck until some burley guy did the, "Hey, kid, get off the truck," thing. As they closed the truck doors Dad, Mother, Patty, and I drove away in our 1951 Ford.

Author; 1955

Aliquippa was named after an Indian queen, Queen Aliquippa. Later on I would discover that Henri Mancini was from there and so was Mike Ditka. And, oh by the way, Joe Namath would play football right across the river in Beaver Falls years later. On the river front of Aliquippa was one of the largest steel mills in the world: Jones & Laughlin Steel, Aliquippa Works, or J&L, or "the mill," and just about the only place to work. The mill was at least five miles long. Five miles! Tons and tons of coal, iron ore, and other raw materials made their way to the mill via trains and barges; that would be very long trains, and very long and very wide gangs of barges. The area was a train mecca and that was fine with me—I liked trains too, but not as much as airplanes.

The plant made everything from coke, iron, steel billets, wheel rims, tin-plated steel, wire, pipe, nails, and lots of byproducts from the coke ovens.

Just south of the plant along the river was the Duquesne Power & Light Company plant. They produced their fair share of smoke and soot along with the mill. Later in my childhood my job would be to sweep the soot off of our very large wraparound porch and very long sidewalk out front. The broom never had to touch the ground. The soot was like black flour. It just blew away—right into my lungs.

When it snowed, it was beautiful; and the next day too. But by the third day the snow on the ground was kind of gray-white, then gray.

After a week or so, if there was no new snow, the cinders they put on the roads (not salt; not invented yet) added to the mix to form black goo. Now I know where the "no white pants after Labor Day" came from.

Our house was on Plan 6, Hill 3 on Laughlin Avenue; 703 Laughlin Avenue. When they first built the town around the turn of the twentieth century the J&L Steel Company built a lot of the houses for the workers, typical for this part of the country. The plan number must have come from the title on the blueprint. Our part of the development, Plan 6, had three hills and we were on the third hill.

We arrived at our new home before the moving van got there. I had a large room and there was an attic with regular stairs, not the pull-down kind. The house had a huge yard and YMCA tennis courts behind the alley in back. What was not to like?

A few days later Mother said we had to go to Pittsburgh to get me shoes and stuff for the "s" word—school. All through my grade school, junior, and senior high school years we had a rule to never say "school" during the summer months.

She and I took the train from Aliquippa to Pittsburgh; the Pittsburgh and Lake Erie Railroad. From the P&LE station we took the bus across the river to downtown Pittsburgh and walked to the two big department stores in Pittsburgh at the time, Horne's and Kaufman's. This was way before malls. The women wore hats with veils; most wore gloves, and some had grotesque dead animals draped around them. Oh, yes, they were furs. For years Mother would say that she had a fur coat too. But it was black and white and hung in the garage due to its funny odor. Every now and then we'd see a lady with a cigarette holder—there was money in Pittsburgh. We didn't have it, but some did. I saw very few men and those I did see all had on ties, hats, and handkerchiefs in their lapel pockets.

Both stores had the same feel. The sound of a gazillion high heels on marble floors, but a library quiet at the same time. Pittsburgh had the first escalators; they were made from wood. There were unmistakable smells of perfumes, colognes, and powders, and those were coming just from the women in the store. The library quiet was cut by the "bong, bong, bong" employee signal codes heard all over the store every breathing minute.

We spent the better part of the day in the store finding clothes for me that I hated, and shoes that I hated.

Since we worked our way upward in the building by escalator Mother decided we should take the elevator down. Oh nooooo, I thought, she's going to do it. I just know it. We entered the crowded elevator after the man holding the lever said, "Going down." He was the elevator operator. He was a black man in a burgundy uniform with epaulets and gold braids, and a nice matching cap. He gripped the elevator drive handle with well worn leather gloves. The door closed… wait for it…wait for it … Then, just before the elevator started down, Mom said, "DIVE…DIVE. OOooggga, OOooggga." And she giggled. I couldn't help but laugh. The delicate net veils turned with baffled looks, clearly not understanding since they had probably never spent time watching a Clark Gable submarine movie with *their* son.

The elevator operator was smiling at us as everyone piled out when we reached the main floor. I think Mother was the highlight of his day. This taught me the power of humor and also to not worry about what others thought. The latter was more difficult for me and came, somewhat, decades later. But I certainly knew where I got my sense of humor and it would serve me all my life.

We exited the elevator, passing the smiling operator with his eyes following my mother. And as the people cleared away, I saw it! Looming above all the lady shoppers, above the perfume counters and above the jewelry was a towering black and white photograph of a B-29 bomber. This just wasn't right; purses, jewelry, yes; but a photo of a B-29 in a department store? No way; what gives?

Mother spotted it the same time I did. She loved airplanes too. Her favorite was the B-25 Mitchell Bomber since we watched *30 Seconds Over Tokyo* with Spencer Tracy together. Later she would be able to identify an F-104 Starfighter, the F-102, the P-38 Lightning, and others. She still had difficulty, however, identifying propeller bombers but she knew she liked the Mitchell. So anytime she saw an American World War II bomber she would ask, "Is that a Mitchell Bomber?" And this occasion was no exception.

"No, Mother, a Mitchell has two engines and two tails. That one has four engines and one tail; it's a B-29." Further details to distinguish a B-29 from a B-17, which also has four engines and one tail, would only confuse the issue.

She was thrilled and I recall how I became even more excited knowing how eager she was to see a picture of an airplane.

"Let's go and see," she said, her eyes gleaming with anticipation.
"OK."

We worked our way through the store and came upon a very large cordoned off area. Big display boards arranged in a zigzag pattern were topped by the B-29 picture that had to be ten feet wide. I saw on the display board lots of smaller photographs, *color* photographs. First, more shots of the B-29; then the B-29 on the ground with lots of people standing in front of it, some shots of atom bomb mushroom clouds, and photos of city rubble. And *then* lots and lots of photos that I examined very closely of Hiroshima and Nagasaki victims. Color photos of skin hanging off of pain-stricken people, bloody blisters and horrible burns, with nurses applying some sort of salve. A photo of a nurse holding a bandage with tongs wrapping oozing burnt flesh …

    that …

        was …

            hanging …

                (fade to black).

I woke up behind the display curtains lying on a couple of wooden folding chairs. When I "came to" I saw an Air Force master sergeant—I recognized the patch on his uniform. He and my mother were apparently not too concerned that I had just passed out. I remember them saying something about me never becoming a doctor.

Yes, ladies and gentlemen, I still have a weak stomach. Even now, if I nick myself with a knife I have ninety seconds to get a Band-Aid or lie down and hang on. Pathetic. But I will never forget not just that USAF department store display of "U.S. Nuclear Strength," but my mother's excitement about airplanes as well. This was a bond for life and it was one of the factors that kept me pointed towards aerospace. Having her and my father's support meant the world to me, even though I didn't fully appreciate it at the time.

* * *

We had a mechanical doorbell that worked by twisting a crank. Sometimes, after being gone for a day or so, we would find the bell dome on the floor inside the house. This was quite a mystery until once when someone came to the door and I heard RING, RING, then THUMP, and then VIZzzzzz, VIZzzzz. That's the sound a crank bell makes with no bell. After they left, I played with the bell mechanism and saw that the ringer loosened and rotated the bell. The bell eventually unscrewed and thumped onto the floor.

One day I heard someone cranking the normal sounding bell. Mother answered the door. She said it was Kent Sargent and to please come downstairs. Who? Oh yeah, he's the kid that gave me the bubble gum in the lumpy letter a couple of weeks ago. I came down the stairs. We instantly became friends, spent many of our school years together, and for many years later we both have figuratively held on to that bubblegum letter and our first meeting. Some people stay in your life forever, even if you only see them every twenty or so years. This is important. It's all about people.

3

In the 1950s extended families lived closer to one another than most do today. We used to go to an aunt or uncle's house just for a visit on a Sunday several times a year. But for Thanksgiving, Christmas, Fourth of July, or other holidays the whole clan showed up at the same time. During these big holidays the tribe numbered about twenty-six people. Mostly we kids and a couple of rug rats raced around whoever's house we were invading.

The journey to visit relatives wasn't too bad, about an hour or less by car. The best thing about the trip was that the road we took went past the Greater Pittsburgh Airport, which had opened a few years earlier. I knew that the end of the runway was very close and perpendicular to a particular spot on the road. The Pennsylvania trees obstructed the airfield but there were a couple of red towers holding the approach lights to the runway on each side of the roadway. Occasionally if we just happened to be at that spot at the right time a very low Connie (Lockheed Constellation) or DC-6 or other type of airplane would fly just yards above our car.

Each time we approached these towers I watched closely and many times we were buzzed by an airplane flying over the threshold. I could easily see the flaps and the gearing for them, the inside of landing gear wells, and streaks of engine and hydraulic oil. I absolutely loved seeing them fly over so low.

* * *

I was almost seven years old; early summer, 1956. My mother told me that my Aunt Toni (short for Anthea) was coming and that we were going to pick her up at the airport on Saturday. WOW! Aunt Toni's coming ... and did someone say *airport*? A few days later we headed out to the Greater Pittsburgh Airport from our house in Aliquippa, which was only a few miles from the end of runway 32.

In fifteen minutes we were walking next to the huge airport fountain just outside the terminal building; it was a fountain where the water "turned colors" at night. Magic.

We went directly to the gate's waiting area. It was small, quiet, and more formal than those of today. There were ash trays on pedestals, and men wearing hats sat in metal art deco-type chairs with green cushions. I ran directly to the window and scanned the airfield. No activity. I looked back into the waiting area and spotted a poster of a TWA Connie—a Lockheed-built four engine, three tail, and gleaming white TWA Constellation passenger plane.

"Hey, mister, is the airplane from California a Connie?"

No answer. Oh yeah, I forgot the adult rule: ignore kid. I went back to the window and saw lights "on final." Finally the ship began to emerge from the distant haze. I saw four engines and lots of wing dihedral. (I even knew that word then.) Then I saw the three tails.

"It's a Connie!" I exclaimed looking back at the people in the waiting room.

Nothing. No response from anyone. Some guy folded over the top corner of his newspaper and looked at me through the stream of smoke rising from the cigarette hanging from his lips. He looked at my mom, who wasn't noticing, looked back at me, then resumed reading.

I saw the Connie approaching. Finally it came in over the runway and touched down onto a puff of white smoke. I lost sight of it, but minutes later it popped into sight again very close to the gate. It was gleaming white and bright silver with TWA proudly displayed on the tail. The two outboard propellers were already stopped. The remaining two were maneuvering the airplane to the gate.

It stopped and rocked on the unmistakably tall nose gear. Activity began: announcements; little carts moved around the plane, and workers pushed stairways to the airplane doors. The propellers stopped and the doors opened. Passengers came out looking like they had just come from church; ladies were wearing hats, furs, and white gloves. All the men had on hats and suits; some carried briefcases. As they came down the stairs, several people fumbled for cigarette packs getting ready to have a smoke once they got inside the gate area. Others waved to greeters.

"There she is," I heard Mother say. Aunt Toni came down the stairs, entered the gate area, and then all the hellos began. Her light-brown hair matched her coat, which was adorned with a fresh corsage. I was excited to see her. Now I got to see who sent me those wonderfully wrapped Christmas presents from California. Finally the hellos and Toni's unmistakable laughter started to die down and I finally got the attention of my aunt (remember kid rule). She came towards me, stooped down, but before she could say anything, I asked excitedly, "So how was it?"

"How was what?" she replied with a big smile.

"How was the Connie?"

"Why, who's she?"

"No, no, the airplane; what was it like to fly in it?" I asked.

"Well ... it was just an airplane."

She exclaimed how much I looked like my dad. (I did.)

I looked back to refocus on the Connie as we walked away from the gate area. How cool it would be to fly in that, I thought.

Never happened. I did build a model of the TWA Connie several decades later to commemorate that day. But what must that have been like? Flying with no onboard movies, loud engines, and unable to fly over some storms– all while dressed in your suit.

4

My first airplane flight was around 1956 with Patty and Grand-daddy, Roy A. Dye Sr., in a DC-3 from Pittsburgh to Toledo on Capital Airlines. Granddaddy wanted to see his son, my father's younger brother, Roy A. Dye Jr. Uncle Roy and Aunt Louise and their several children lived near Toledo. I guess he thought it would be fun to bring Patty and me along.

I was excited beyond anything I had experienced in my short life. Being *inside* the airplane when the engines started, experiencing the takeoff, and looking out the window as we flew through the clouds was exhilarating. They gave us a meal too, complete with a small four pack of cigarettes that Patty and I took out and pretended we were smoking until the stewardess politely grabbed them from us.

I absolutely loved my first airplane ride and it whetted my appetite for more. But the next commercial flight I took wasn't until I flew an Allegheny 727 to Philly from Pittsburgh in a snow storm in '68; but that's another story.

* * *

Patty was about three years older than me and we got along quite well, most of the time. We did lots of things together as kids. We played games, read books about dinosaurs, and along with some of our neighbors formed the Junior Woodchuck Club.

One day I walked downtown to our main street, Franklin Avenue. It was summer, a perfect day, hot but not too humid. The 1950s buses had their windows open and heat waves wafted up from the hot streets. A few men stood wiping their brows as another forced a clattering jack hammer into a corner of the avenue. The State Movie Theater marquee was in transition. A ladder remained as evidence of a job to be finished when it was cooler.

A few blocks more and I would reach Murphy's dime store where, a few years earlier, I had discovered plastic models and just about everything else a kid needed. It had a sign out front that said "air conditioned." Painted icicles hung from each letter illustrating just how cool it was inside. Murphy's wasn't a hobby shop by any means. There was just one small section in the store with the plastic model kits, tubes of glue (displayed and sold openly before the other features of said glue were discovered), and maybe packages of Testors paints.

I looked at the plastic kit boxes: Revell, Lindberg, Comet, Aurora, and others. A Revell box that had a rather good illustration of a B-36 bomber caught my eye. It was shown in flight; six propellers mounted behind the wings with white contrails streaming from jet pods. It reminded me of an arcade card I got at Kenneywood Park near Pittsburgh for a penny.

Box cover of Revell B-36 plastic kit
Courtesy of Revell Corporation

I had to have this. I dug deep into my pockets and fished out two weeks' allowance—fifty cents—along with some lint covered, but still good, penny candy and three cat's eye marbles. The sales lady gave me some change, enough for a couple packs of baseball cards, Topps, at the candy store, but that was several blocks away; maybe another time. She slid the model into a brown paper bag along with a small receipt. Once again I passed under the icicle sign and began my hike back up the hill toward home.

As I approached our house I stopped just short of the front porch steps. My exhilaration grew as I pulled the box out of the bag. In moments I would start to build this beast. A maple tree shaded the box, and the smell of my mother's flowers nearly diverted my attention. I slipped the model back into the bag and as I climbed the blue-gray porch steps they squeaked under my then small frame.

Excitedly I called my mother. She stooped down. I felt her hand on my shoulder and as she admired my purchase she said, "Wow! Look at that. It's a pusher!" Because the propellers were behind the wing's trailing edge they were called pushers. How many moms would know *that*? Within a few hours I was painting the spinners and the jet engine intakes bright red just like on the box.

Many years later my mother would tell people, "He had a B-36 pusher prop model put together before I was done reading the directions!"

It was the excitement that I remember the most. Models brought my awareness closer to my dream of flying, and maybe even to becoming a test pilot. The more models I bought and built the closer I felt to airplanes. Models allow you to own a three-dimensional image of whatever you want around you. It's almost like collecting the real thing. Obviously it isn't, I mean there's reality, but you can collect your favorite airplanes, ships, rockets, or whatever. It was fun. And it was inexpensive.

I built a model of the bright red Snark 1950s cruise missile, one of the Matador, another cruise missile of the '50s, science fiction models, Werner Von Braun and Willie Ley speculative spaceships like the Revell XSL-01 and the Space Taxi. There was a Thor IRBM missile, an Atlas missile complete with launching pad, a Hawk brand kit of the Corporal missile, a giant white Lindberg kit of the Douglas Skyray Navy jet, a few ships like a destroyer that Dad helped me paint, and the USS *Forrestal* aircraft carrier.

There were many more. I wish I had them now not only for their value but just for the memories, especially that destroyer. Dad very carefully masked off the hull with tape and painted the bottom of the hull red. He stripped off the tape and like magic the red water level was a perfectly straight line. This was an attempt to show me how the battleship I had finished a month earlier and painted by hand could be even better if I took the time to put on a piece of masking tape. It worked; I learned.

My collection began to grow and after a few years, when I was around nine years old, Mother and I put up a pegboard on a wall in my bedroom. We made coat hanger wire struts and mounted all of my models in flying attitudes, well, the airplanes anyway. She liked my models too. I cherished her support for my interest in airplanes and science.

Proud author displays models; 1959

* * *

I was in third grade when Granddaddy took me to the Air National Guard unit stationed at the Greater Pittsburgh Airport. It was 1958. They had F-86 Sabre jets, F-84 Thunderstreaks, and T-33 Shooting Stars. I was in heaven. The man that was showing us around must have been pretty high up because everyone was saluting him. He had a lot of shiny things on his uniform. His hat had lots of stuff on it too. It occurred to me, at eight years old, that the more shiny stuff you had on your uniform the higher up you were, or so it seemed.

He showed us the flight line and I marveled at the gleaming jets before me. We walked over to one of the newer F-86Ds, a radar-equipped Sabre jet, and he asked if I would like to sit in the cockpit. Would I! Some ground crew guys were trying to put my little feet, in my US Keds, into the jet airplane fuselage push-in hand holds—strategically placed for adult hands and feet to climb into the cockpits. "Hold on!" they exclaimed. My heart pounded. I was climbing into my dream. I sat in the pilot's seat and looked at all of the dials and switches; I imagined feeling the Gs as I made hard turns with the jet whine in my ears. My mind was at twenty thousand feet.

They coaxed me out of the cockpit and as we walked across the flight line back to the buildings I could see the impressive line of Sabre jet tails. I wanted one of them to be my airplane. While I was craning my neck to view the jets one last time, the man said, "Don't worry, we'll come back so you can see more jets. I want to show you something I think you'll like."

We went into an old building with many different rooms all looking very important and certainly housing serious stuff. In the hallway were lots of clipboards, photos of more guys with lots of shiny things on their uniforms, and blackboards with all kinds of things meticulously written on them. He directed us through a doorway into a curiously small room that housed a cockpit. I knew instantly it was from an F-86D Sabre jet. There was an airman inside the Sabre simulator with headphones on. I noticed that he had far less stuff on his uniform and he really moved when our guy said, "Would you mind if we slipped in here?" He picked me up and put me into the cockpit, placed the headphones on my head, and told me I could fly. WOW!

"What do I do?" I asked.

"Anything you want."

I remembered you had to ask for permission to takeoff. So I did. I heard a voice over the headphones say, "November Papa 35 cleared for takeoff."

"Roger," I said.

Suddenly the cockpit came to life. Dials moved, I heard sounds, and lights blinked on and off. A little later I heard him say to push the red button on the control stick to fire missiles; I missed. Then he said to push the button when the "X" appeared on the radar screen. I did, and I shot down an enemy plane! Hu-huu!

Of course, the "general" told me I did better than his airmen, who were patiently waiting with smiles on their faces. Of course, I believed him.

* * *

It took days for me to climb down from cloud nine. I felt so lucky to have been given the opportunity to experience a taste of what I dreamed of doing. So now, I just had to build a jet simulator like the one I got to "fly." Mom had an old bureau that she didn't want down in the basement. I took out all the drawers, flipped it on its back, covered it with pieces of cardboard to make it look more authentic, and made an instrument panel out of a piece of scrap Masonite. I found some lights my dad had in the basement, plus a mayonnaise jar full of toggle switches that Mr. Cunningham from church gave him. Mr. Cunningham told us that the switches came from a B-25. Appropriate.

I drilled holes in the Masonite, mounted the lights and the B-25 switches, and wired them up. I hooked it all up to my dad's train transformer and flicked a switch; the lights actually went on. No smoke. It worked. Oh, by the way, some people actually think that electronics and electrical circuits run on electricity or rather flowing electrons. Not so. They run on smoke. Once smoke comes out, it doesn't work anymore. And NO one is smart enough to capture the smoke to put it back in; it comes out when you *least* expect it. See, it can't be just any ordinary smoke, it's gotta be the original smoke that's inside each electronic part. Years later this theory held up in testing satellite flight hardware.

I made a separate control panel for another guy to turn on warning lights for things like "fire" and "low hydraulic pressure," inspired by the 1955 movie *The McConnell Story*. My next door neighbor, James Findley (I called him Finney) and I played fighter pilot all summer in that thing, bailing out over enemy territory after a warning light like "flameout" came on, but scampering home just in time for dinner.

5

Mom and Dad told me that I was to spend some time at my grandfather's apartment in Sewickley, Pennsylvania, across the Ohio River from us. I didn't know why; maybe they wanted some peace and quiet for a week. Patty went to a cousin's house. I really wasn't too thrilled about this because my relationship with my grandfather was—how shall I say it?—strained.

Granddaddy had taken Patty to movies in Pittsburgh several times, but never me. He just told me to read *Huckleberry Finn* and discouraged me from reading "all that airplane and space nonsense." He was still harping on this several years later when I was in high school and my mother had a few choice words for him; it didn't help. Later, in college, I would find the value in reading that book, and later on I enjoyed other Mark Twain stories, but it took some doing to get me to read it.

My parents told me I would have to spend nearly a week with Granddaddy. So I packed up my "space nonsense" books, a plastic model or two, and my bicycle, which my grandfather had given me the year before for my birthday. He lived in an apartment complex that was about as exciting for kids as a hospital with no TVs. It had a sidewalk that was laid out in a giant square so I rode my bike around and around the square until even I couldn't stand it.

When I came inside, I read a book on the Thor missile. And to pass the time I drew sketches of rockets while I sat at Granddaddy's dining table; he had no TV.

Later, being very careful not to get glue on his table, I built a few plastic models. He asked, "What are you going to do with those?" and I said, "Mother will help me put them on my pegboard." He just stared at me with obvious judgment churning inside of him. I could easily

20

read his thoughts: So what's the purpose of this again? or Why are you doing this?

I remember thinking, I bet if I painted a nice scene or someone's portrait on a canvas and hung it on the wall, that would be OK. So how come if I build a plastic airplane and put it on the wall that's not OK? No one says to an artist, "But it doesn't do anything; it just sits on the wall."

Looking back I realize that I could "read" people with great accuracy. This paid off in my adult years and really helped when I was a manager. You learn when people don't agree with you but say they do, or when they're BS'ing you or flat-out lying. Maybe I should have played poker.

Granddaddy was retired from J&L Steel. He was a big shot there and was the manager of the Personnel and Labor Relations Department. He was typical 1950s old school. He'd had his larynx removed in the '40s or '50s due to cancer. There was a hole in his throat and he had to clear it frequently. He would visit our house every Sunday, and, yes, Mother would make a seven-course meal every time. During the meal he inevitably wanted to tell a joke. He talked by burping; take a deep breath, burp/talk, deeeeeep breath, and burp/talk. A little joke turned into a shaggy dog story very quickly. But we were polite and we laughed.

During my long stay with him, I noticed a *Life* magazine in his magazine holder. I was quite bored so I began thumbing through the pages. I landed on an ad describing "the airport of the future." The article said the Los Angeles International Airport would have jet ways that would allow passengers to board and exit futuristic all-jet airplanes without being exposed to the weather. I never forgot that photo and it was just one example of the excitement about the future of aerospace during that time.

Finally my parents came to pick me up; they had been gone for what seemed like 670 years. It was my space books, my plastic models, my sketches of rockets, and day dreaming of flying that got me through that very long week. Looking back on my grandfather now, I believe he simply did not know how to relate to kids. He tried. He *did* take me to the National Guard and that fueled the fire of my longing to fly jets. He did take me on one or two fishing trips, and he did give me a bicycle for my birthday. Plus, he did give me some good advice—to read good books.

But he wanted me to do or to be interested in what he thought I should be doing or whatever he was interested in, rather than what *I* wanted to do. I got the feeling that he was thinking more about my future with respect to money and, most of all, "making it." Aerospace, in his mind, was not a good business and not a place to earn money. For the most part he was right, but I did OK in the end.

As a spin-off of this, I often wondered about kids who didn't have a clue about what they wanted to be or do. I just couldn't imagine that. My mother and father did everything they could to support my interests. Throughout the years for birthdays or for Christmas they would buy me science stuff like a microscope with prepared slides, a chemistry set, and lots of chemistry glassware—that was cool—a telescope, space books, and a Hasbro jet simulator. I had my space and airplane interests to push me through school and beyond. I was lucky, I guess. I knew what I wanted to do. I wanted to fly jets.

6

It was 1959, summer. I was almost ten. Western Pennsylvania is quite hilly, part of the Appalachian Mountains. Mother asked me to go downtown for bread, and since I was used to this hike, I didn't mind the chore. Besides, I could stop at Murphy's Five and Dime store and look for a new model to build if I had enough allowance money.

On my way to Isaly's, a store where we got milk and bread—and yes, it had a real soda fountain—I saw a large blue truck. It was a moving van-sized trailer parked in front of the post office with about a dozen people milling about. I wasn't sure whether to go over or not. The last van I saw like that had an electric chair display. Stained leather straps on a chair like I'd never seen before and never want to again. Dad took me.

But I was curious and decided to go over to see what was in this van that seemed to be attracting so much attention. As I approached I saw U.S.A.F. printed high on the front. Hey, what could this be? I wondered. I turned the corner and could see the whole van. It was some sort of United States Air Force traveling road show.

I made a beeline to the entrance and climbed the special wooden stairs, painted Air Force blue, of course. The first thing I saw was a master sergeant, who looked at me and smiled. When I saw his stripes it reminded me of the A-bomb pictures in that department store in Pittsburgh. I shook it off because I had a hunch there wouldn't be any gory pictures in this display.

Behind him were really cool photos of airplanes and signs like Peace Is Our Profession, plus pictures of F-86s, F-94C fighters firing rockets, a rocket-assisted B-47 taking off with black smoke pouring out of the rocket-assisted takeoff (RATO) rockets, and then I saw it … a *huge* picture of a Republic F-84F Thunderstreak with all kinds of bombs, rockets, fuel tanks, and machine gun belts laid out in front of it, plus a guy wearing a G-suit and helmet standing amongst the ordnance. When I saw all of those things the F-84 could carry—well, not all at once—I thought it was dynamite. That photo was indelibly burned into my mind and, to me, it represented our "air power"; I wanted to be a part of that.

U. S. air power
Courtesy of USAF

Little did I know that many years later a different photograph would depict the pinnacle of my aerospace career, and I would compare it to this photo of the F-84 that spurred my interest in aerospace.

* * *

One evening during that same summer my mother and dad were reading the newspaper, the *Pittsburgh Press*. I was on the floor watching TV. In the evening my parents hid behind two sheets of newspaper that rustled occasionally. Mother suddenly said very excitedly, "Oooh, Be-ill (that's how it sounded instead of Bill) there's going to be a Boeing 707 at the Greater Pittsburgh Airport this weekend. Says here it's the debut of the very first American all-jet commercial airliner, and it's touring the country." She folded the paper over and said, "Let's go! Ham?" (My dad was called "Ham," short for Hamilton.) He said, "Sure!" Actually, he was quite well known for saying "sure" a lot, a habit I learned to mimic years later with scary accuracy.

That Saturday we went to the Greater Pittsburgh Airport, and as we walked from the parking lot past the fountain, I spotted the top of a tall white fin above the fence. I knew DC-6 and DC-7 fins; they were curved and certainly wouldn't be visible from the parking lot. This fin was tall with straight edges and had a probe of some sort on the top. Oh man, this thing must be big, I thought.

We passed all of the limousines that were parked at the curb and the valet parking stand, and went into the terminal to the observation deck. I opened the door, ran out to the guard rail, and leaned over. There it was: a gleaming TWA Boeing 707 jet airliner, with swept-back wings, turbojet engines—beautiful! This was absolutely incredible. It was like looking at something out of Buck Rogers, the 1950s TV series about a space cadet fighting evil with his crew aboard his rocket ship.

I had never seen a swept-wing airplane this big; I'd only seen pictures of B-47s and B-52s. The top of the 707 was white with the unmistakable TWA red "rocket" paint scheme on the side over the windows. The bottom was gleaming polished aluminum.

There were two sets of stairs, one set aft and one at the front of the aircraft. There was a line of people going up the stairs and a few, every now and then, coming out of the front. "The paper said we can go inside. Let's go!" Mother exclaimed.

"Sure!" Dad said with a big smile on his face, his pipe hanging from his mouth.

We went downstairs and followed the signs; before we knew it we were on the tarmac. So this is what it would be like getting onto a huge jet airliner if I were a passenger, I thought. I climbed the stairs and went inside the aft door. It was beautiful. There was three-and-three seating with little white headrest towels on each seat. The seats seemed nice too. Some of the tables were down and you could see the ashtrays in the armrests. There were TWA logos on everything. We walked the entire length of the aircraft. There was only enough time to glance at the cockpit. I saw the countless gauges and switches and wanted so much to sit in the pilot seat. But we were ushered out.

After we climbed down the TWA stairs I stood just watching, examining this beautiful piece of machinery. My parents and Patty had had enough so I agreed to go home.

Two days later, I was on the floor again watching TV and from behind the newspaper my mother laughed and said, "Looks like people stripped the Boeing 707 we went to see on Saturday."

"Really? What do you mean?" I asked.

"Says here they took ashtrays, magazines, the white head towels, anything they could; TWA had to make some repairs…looks like it will leave this Saturday."

"What time?"

"They don't say."

Days later, Saturday morning, about six o'clock, I went outside. For years I had watched Connies, DC-6s, DC-7s, Vickers Viscounts, and DC-3s fly right over our house, so I thought this would be no different. I'd get to see for the first time a Boeing 707 jetliner fly right over our house.

I waited. When I got tired of standing I sat on the milk box. The milk box was an insulated box that kept the milk cold. Back then milk was delivered to your house. The milkman put the glass milk bottles in and took the empties out when he made deliveries, usually once or twice a week; and, yes, he wore a uniform.

I sat on the box. It moved a little, rattling the few empties inside. At noon Mother brought me a sandwich. I ate it and waited some more. And I waited. Around 3:00 p.m., after sitting on the milk box for nine hours, I heard a roar like faraway thunder but constant. Then I heard a high-pitched whine on top of that. Our "hill" was between me and the sound, so the horizon was rather high. The sound grew louder and suddenly I saw it, the huge jet airplane, swept wings silhouetted against the overcast sky and black smoke pouring from the four screaming engines. It was still pretty low, probably a thousand feet, and it flew directly overhead. I ran out into our backyard so I could see it as it went over the house. It banked to the right revealing the top of the jet in its steep turn, black smoke tracing its route. It climbed into the dreary gray clouds and I waited for minutes until the sound was gone.

A few minutes later a propeller-driven DC-6 flew over. The comparison was like night and day. Standing there in the backyard straining to watch the diminishing smoke trail of the 707, I knew I was witnessing the future. This was the jet, rocket, and space age and I was determined to be a part of it.

* * *

I liked science in general but I read everything I could find about the space program, launch vehicles, and missiles. With my allowance and a contribution from my parents, I subscribed to Science Service books, and once a month or so they sent me a small paperback on different science subjects. Each had color plates in the center of the book that you were to cut out and paste in the appropriate space in the book. Now I realize how much cheaper it was to publish these that way. "Let the kid do the pasting; it'll make them feel like they're doing something," which turned out to be true, at least in my case.

For a while I also subscribed to the National Weather Service and for about a buck a month they sent me daily weather maps of the United States. Good pilots had to know about weather, right? I had so many maps I could have papered the house. I used them a few years later as drawing paper for rocket designs. I bought an "electronic" weathervane and anemometer—the wind speed gizmo with little cups that whirled around and around—and mounted it outside the attic window; the wire came through a notch I filed into the window sash.

For my twelfth birthday Mom gave me a hardbound book entitled *Mike Mars*. The dust jacket had a guy in a fighter jet cockpit wearing a USAF helmet. I read it hanging onto every word. It was the first of several child novels by Donald A. Wollheim about an Air Force pilot, Mike Mars, who wants to become an astronaut. This and other books followed his progress from flying F-100 Super Sabres to the Project Mercury Space Program, the Gemini Program, and other projects, all with references to the ongoing Cold War. It was pure propaganda for the U.S. Air Force and NASA, but I ate it up.

Mike Mars told us kids that we should have a plan; you need to study, do well, and you too can be a test pilot, or whatever you want to be. The plan was like climbing a ladder one rung at a time; first school, then college, then pilot training.

I just couldn't get enough of those stories. I got the entire series, four I think, as they came out. Three or four more were published but I never got those. I wanted to fly jets and I made my Mike Mars plan. Following it might be called a stretch, but at least I had a goal.

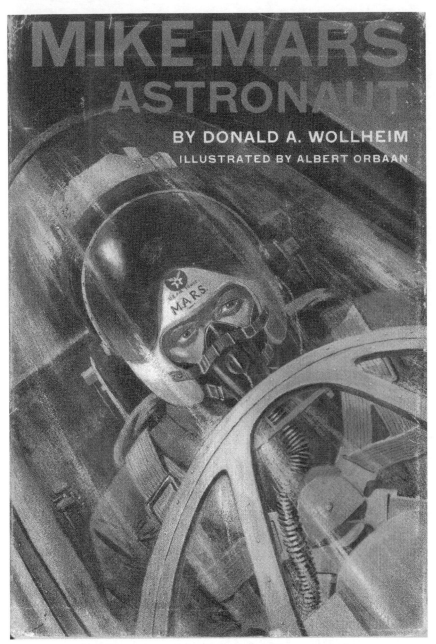

Mike Mars told us we should have a plan
Courtesy Doubleday Publishing Company

7

Mother and I took another of our many trips to Pittsburgh to the eye doctor. On one occasion we got there at ten o'clock for our 10:45 a.m. appointment. We waited; 11:30, noon, nothing. Finally she asked the nurse if we could go get lunch since the doctor was running late.

"No," she snapped. She was rather crabby.

To pass the time, I read one of the books on space travel that I got from school. It was about the Mariner Spacecraft and various interplanetary missions. I also brought a *National Geographic* that the cleaning lady at school gave me. Her daughter was in my class and had told her mother I liked airplanes and space stuff, so she gave it to me. Nice lady. It was the "50-Year Anniversary of Flight" issue with a formation of Republic F-105s on the cover. Inside, one of the photos was of a guy tethered by a cable that suspended him in front of an F-84 jet intake with streamers attached to him showing how the jet engine was trying to suck him in. Try that today. There were all kinds of pictures showing how far we had come in fifty years since the Wright brothers.

Finally at 2:30 p.m. a lady in white came into the waiting area and called "Billy Dye" as loud as she could. By now we were on a first-name basis with all the other waiting patients.

Once inside the doctor's office we did the normal eye chart thing with the little black paddle over each eye and the little handheld light thingy. "Follow the light with your eyes."

I sometimes thought, What else would I follow with? My foot? Then he handed me a picture of a fly and asked if it looked flat or if it seemed to be popping out of the paper. Was this a trick question? It was printed on a piece of paper, flat paper, two-dimensional flat paper.

How could it be 3-D to even a "normal" person? His arrogant attitude really irritated me.

"It's flat," I said.

He very curtly replied, "You have no depth perception; therefore, you'll never fly jets. Here, take this slip of paper to the receptionist." I thought he was going to yell out "next."

When we got home I told my dad what had happened with this guy and he agreed to get a second opinion. So we made another trip to Pittsburgh a few weeks later. Denial prevailed. We went to see Dr. Hoon. And this time I was with Dad—not that Mom couldn't handle it, but I think he took a day off work to show his support for my interest in flying. And, he said he wanted to "get to the bottom of this."

We waited only five minutes. I had barely cracked one of the five books I'd brought with me. Dr. Hoon was nice and he didn't talk down to us. He very clearly explained how I didn't have something in my brain (my mother mentioned that to me often) that took both images from my eyes and fused them together to produce a 3-D image. He did some tests—not the fly on the paper—and concluded that I had strabismus and was an "alternator." That meant I looked out of one eye at a time. I saw double all the time. Well, yeah, doesn't everybody? He said that my brain gets 'tired' of seeing two images and so it blocks one out; it blocks the image from the eye that's not in use. So I could switch from one eye to another. Whichever eye I was looking out of, well, the other eye would turn in, a lot. What a babe magnet. High school was going to be a blast. I just couldn't wait.

He thought I would be able to fly private airplanes, but he doubted that I could pass the Air Force exam for flight training. He seemed very sad that he had to confirm the other doctor's diagnosis. I liked that.

So at twelve, my dream of flying jets was confirmed over. I was absolutely devastated. Deep down I guess I always knew that this would be the outcome; I mean, how many pilots do you see with their eyes out of whack? But having it official was like a punch in my stomach. I got home, looked at my models, and sobbed. I felt lost, with no direction.

Funny, though, how it never occurred to me that I could be a navigator or flight engineer. Maybe it was just an ego thing, like you see in the movies about guys who wash out of pilot training and are sent to navigator's school. "I want to be the guy at the controls," they'd say.

I never saw myself as a control freak; instead, I wonder if giving up was easier than considering the various other opportunities for flying; maybe I had that "everything is either white or black" kind of thing. It took me several years to start considering compromises.

So, at twelve, even though the news that I already knew deep down was bad, I still had the airplane bug. But maybe rocketry would be the ticket. I had always had a great interest in them too. So, I thought it would be a great idea to build a rocket. I did some reading in the library and the books said I needed gunpowder, a key component needed to make a rocket. I went down to the hardware store on Franklin Avenue, approached the counter where they sold guns, stood on my tippy toes, and told the man behind the counter, in the deepest voice I could muster, that I wanted some black powder.

"Why?" he asked.

"Well, I'm going to build a rocket and I need black powder to do it."

He looked me up and down and then said, "OK." I bet he thought, Egghead … harmless. So I came home with a tin of powder.

Unfortunately (or fortunately), I told my parents and they seemed just a tad concerned. Dad had a chat with the Aliquippa Senior High School science teacher, Mr. Fazio, and they decided it would be in the best interest of the free world to remove the tin of powder from the hands of this babe. But he did invite Dad and me to the Aliquippa Senior High Science Club picnic, where some of the eons-older students were going to launch a rocket made with homemade propellant. They even said to bring my rocket, which was an aluminum tube with a cap threaded on the end.

We went to the picnic, Dad with his pipe, long coat, and 1950s-style hat; me with wacko eyes, glasses, and an aluminum tube. There were lots of kids there. They had a few telescopes set up and the cool guys were ogling the babes and "showing them" how to look through the telescope. It began to dawn on me why the science club picnic was popular—and I'd thought it was about science! I got to see Saturn through the telescope of some guy that wasn't exactly a babe magnet, unlike me of course. Then someone came out on the field of telescopes and asked, "Where's the kid with the rocket?"

"Here I am," I declared. I could have sworn I heard a giggle. Nah, must have been the wind.

"Come on with me; I'm gonna mix propellant." Dad was ten feet behind us, with his smoking pipe. This guy, who looked like me except a lot older, started to mix something in a wooden mixing bowl. It was zinc dust and sulfur. His rocket was huge, nearly four feet long lying on the table with its fins hanging over the edge. The motor was only a few inches long; it was some kind of a miniature tank, and it was already filled about three-fourths of the way with another type of propellant. He filled it the rest of the way with the propellant he was mixing in the salad bowl. Hmm, I thought, this should be interesting. The leftover propellant in the bowl filled up my "rocket."

We took both rockets to the launching area, the teacher's back yard, and he propped up my very un-sexy rocket and lit the fuse. Everyone scrambled and it lit up with a hiss and then a louder hiss. It hissed and hissed and hissed as it shrunk smaller and smaller into oblivion; the aluminum tube melted away. We made a flare. I thought I heard, "I'm mellllting, I'm mellllting..." Nah, the wind again.

This thing about having a nozzle was known by yours truly; I just didn't have one. And our cracker jack high school student and wannabe rocket scientist didn't mix the correct proportions, let alone notice there was no nozzle. But, hey, what did I know, right? I'm just the dorky kid.

He put the bigger rocket on a makeshift launch rail and lit the fuse. It hissed for a second with the crappy propellant he'd mixed; then it hit the good stuff and whoooosh! It took off. Having fins, it flew pretty straight; it went up about two hundred feet, turned over, and came straight down. Everyone took off. I could see it was going to land almost two hundred feet away (he had a very big yard). When it hit, it sunk into the ground about a foot.

I realized that I wasn't old enough to be mixing my own propellant so rockets would have to wait. I would consider it again a few years later. But my parents were still not convinced that even a few years later I could safely make rocket propellant. These rockets were not toys. Maybe in *several* years.

8

We **went on a** two-week vacation every year. Not one year was missed during my childhood; not one. A few times we went to Atlantic City, New Jersey—well, Wildwood really. It was my introduction to blue snow cones as well as rides on the Wild Mouse roller-coaster with my dad; I was eight or nine.

When I was eleven Mother decided that she, and therefore we, wanted to go to Florida. She saved every dime for the Florida trip and plans were being made in March. She wrote Chambers of Commerce, got hotel information, and made reservations by mail. There was no internet and long distance calls happened, well, never, not even if someone died. Planning the trip was quite an undertaking back then, but she did it.

While she was planning, I was riveted to all of the space stuff. The whole country was starting to catch space fever. I was no exception and neither was Mother.

I stayed home from school and watched Alan Shepard's historical first space flight. The school bureaucrats wanted to say it was an unexcused absence. Mother called and read them the riot act. "This is history in the making. Why don't you think that's education?" she chided. They caved. Shepard's flight was in May 1961. I watched live as he gazed up at the rocket after he got out of the van on the launching pad. Hours later, I saw the impressive, white-knuckle liftoff, followed by the capsule recovery only fifteen minutes later. All of this was narrated by Walter Cronkite.

Grissom was next. He was scheduled to go in July. Those were the days; a shot every few weeks or months. A paperback book came out all about Project Mercury and the astronauts. And that one went along with me to the eye doctor.

School was finally out, and a few weeks later on a warm night in July I helped Dad pack the car. We would be leaving for Florida the next day. We packed clothes, fishing rods, swimsuits, cooking utensils, and other stuff until well after my bedtime.

After only a few hours' sleep we left before the sun came up and drove to the Pennsylvania turnpike. When we got to the Breezewood exit we turned south heading toward Florida. For years Mother would talk about the Breezewood exit because it reminded her of this Florida trip.

After getting off of the Pennsy turnpike all the roads were two lanes; there were no freeways. Every afternoon we stopped for an hour or so to swim and cool down since cars didn't have air conditioning then. We stayed in little motels with the typical 1950s metal lawn chairs that are now in vogue. Mother made peanut butter sandwiches and peanut butter cookies in advance and packed them in tins; we ate them all the way to Tampa. I think I've had only six peanut butter cookies since then.

Florida was great. We went to Treasure Island south of St. Petersburg. I think part of the trip was to be a surprise—to go watch the Grissom launch. But the weather was bad and they decided to start back north. On our way back we went up through Cypress Gardens, some alligator farm, Jacksonville, Fort Lauderdale and eventually to Norfolk, Virginia. That stop was planned because there was a Navy base there. We did go on the tour and I got to see some "gate guard" airplanes; they were airplanes on stands, for display. One was an experimental vertical takeoff and landing aircraft with contra-rotating props. My mother said, "Oooh, Be-ill, there's a V-T-O-L." I was impressed. She held the dream for me too. Patty just stared out the window, not enthused about all of this. But later she and I got back into Rock, Scissors, Paper and all was well with the world.

That night we stayed in a very small cottage right on the Chesapeake Bay; well, across the road from the shore. The next day we all sat around the kitchen table and listened to the launch of Gus Grissom, the second American in space, on a little two-transistor radio I bought in Florida. We listened to space history. This was the first year of the United States' manned space program. We all felt a part of it; even if only through that tiny radio.

When we got home I began cataloging the space shots, manned or unmanned. Mother saved newspapers with all of the important headlines. And I started to peer at the stars and the planets through a telescope I'd received a few years before on my tenth birthday. Little did I know what the future would hold for me with respect to telescopes and space.

9

Since Dad worked in personnel and labor relations at the Aliquippa J&L Steel plant, he met lots of people in the "mill." One was a pilot, a private pilot. He somehow wrangled a way to have this guy invite me for a ride—and I would get to fly the plane. After reading about aircraft instruments in the encyclopedia, a book entitled *Flight Instruments* given to me by Mr. Cunningham from church, and several library books on flying, I knew the instruments and the basic principles of controlling an airplane. Our TV was the old tunable type—no remote; you tuned in the channels by turning knobs. There was a spot where I could listen to the Greater Pittsburgh Airport control tower and I started to learn the jargon for talking on the radio.

I studied navigation and the different radio systems that let the pilot know if he was to the left or right of a station, a ground point with a transmission tower. Other systems you could dial into the frequency and it gave you a reference bearing or a distance from you to it.

So one Saturday afternoon this man, we'll call him Phil, and I drove to the Beaver County Airport, about ten miles northwest of Aliquippa. We went into the office and he signed out a "Stinson" airplane, an old fabric high-wing single engine tail dragger. The airplane rental guy said, "Weather's pretty crappy; keep the airport in sight." It was overcast with off and on drizzle. He also said, "Make a 'long' landing because we're repairing the end of the runway and there are some yellow sawhorses set up at the end."

We went to the airplane. I was excited but anxious at the same time; I didn't really know this guy. He showed me the navigation devices explaining stuff, most of which I already knew a fair amount about, but I was polite. And besides, seeing the instruments in the flesh was a lot more intriguing than in the encyclopedia.

I followed him as he did the walk-around; then we got into the plane and he started the engine. It warmed up for a while and we taxied to, but held short of, the runway. He showed me how to do the magneto check and we went through a checklist; I was a copilot! He opened the throttle and we rolled down the runway. Before I knew it we were airborne. Phil let me take the control wheel and before long I was flying—and wanting to go higher and higher.

After a few turns and within five minutes we lost sight of the airport. Then it started to rain, very hard. This was starting to look like not such a great idea. He did a one-eighty to get out of the rain. That worked for a while but then we hit even more rain. I was looking down at all of the western Pennsylvania tree-covered hills while he was looking for landmarks. Then I heard the dreaded words, "Look for a place to land!"

On what? The treetops? Are you nuts?! But what came out of me was, "OK." He looked at the map, tried to fly, looked out the window, tried to fly, looked at the map, out the window, and scratched the side of his face. Finally I said, "How about you fly and I'll navigate." His eyes were the diameter of B-29 props. "OK," he said and handed me, the twelve-year-old kid, the map. I found a dome light on the ceiling and opened the map. I recognized Pittsburgh and then found some other towns I was familiar with, so I "had my bearings" (with the map anyway). There were radio frequency numbers next to the Greater Pittsburgh and New Castle airports on the map. It was the frequency for the OMNI range-bearing indicator that he'd briefed me on before we took off.

I got the bearing from each airport; I figured out our position and then said, "Turn left to two three zero degrees," just like in the movies. The rain pounded on the windshield. He turned the plane without question or wavering. I knew I didn't account for the time it took to get both readings, and that fact we were traveling at an angle away from our location on the map. I could have done it again, but figured we'd be "in the ballpark."

We were going about 85 mph or so, and looking at the map I

guessed we were about ten miles away. I did the math and said, "Should be just off the nose to the right in a few minutes."

A few minutes later we saw the flashing airport beacon. It was just off the nose to the left. I'd missed by about a half mile. Not too shabby, I thought.

He entered the pattern and turned onto final approach. Flaps down. We drew closer and closer to the ground. I could see the runway ahead through the drizzling rain. Suddenly, full throttle, we jerked up—just missing some sawhorses with blinking lights on them, but touching down a few hundred feet later. Oh yeah, "Make a long landing" came back to me.

We landed, taxied in, and he thanked me for my help. I got out and mentally kissed the ground. But I was pretty proud of my young self. I had navigated us out of a rain storm. I'd like to do that again, but not with Phil.

I was captivated by this experience. It fueled the flames of having *something* to do with aerospace. My entry into the world of space and science was about to take off.

* * *

Americans' space fever heated up even more than before. There were science fiction movies and the TV series *Men into Space,* which showed wheel-like space stations. Even Sputnik bubble gum—powder blue balls covered with crystallized sugar—appeared on the market. Laundromats, cafes, and bars with "rocket" in their titles cropped up, and these establishments were usually accompanied by some ridiculous neon rocket sign. Even cars wanted to be jet airplanes with hood ornaments that looked like futuristic jet planes.

During the school year we were given the opportunity to buy small paperback books from a catalog they passed out. They had a book on the X-15 rocket plane and others. Dad gave me money for these and I couldn't wait for them to arrive. I usually got a stack of them and it bolstered my egghead reputation at school, even though my grades weren't the greatest. The X-15 book was so exciting to me. I saw newspaper articles on it and perhaps a *Life* magazine article.

I found a model kit for a very small B-52 at Murphy's. With the book and now the B-52 model, I had an idea for my seventh grade science project. I mounted the B-52 model, built a small model of the X-15 from scratch, and depicted the flight path of the X-15 over the California desert and mountains. Lights showed the launching area, the tracking stations, and the landing area.

The X-15 was a research plane designed to push the envelope with respect to altitude and Mach number (speed measured in units of the speed of sound). It was carried aloft under the right wing of a special B-52 bomber, the NB-52A. The NB-52A took the X-15 up to between thirty thousand and forty thousand feet where it was "dropped." After release, the X-15 pilot fired the rocket engines accelerating the rocket plane to incredible altitudes and speeds. It even went into space, higher than one hundred miles, and set the record for the fastest airplane at Mach 6.

The school liked the project so much I had to take it to classes other than science class and make "show and tell" presentations. So I became known as "Bill Dye the Science Guy," with black horn-rimmed glasses to boot. And I started to enjoy making presentations; this would certainly come in handy years later.

* * *

The next year I had completed a plastic model of a nuclear submarine that was "cut away" so that you could see the compartments inside, such as torpedo rooms, control rooms, living quarters, engine room, and coning tower. Mother, being very creative, suggested that I build a cut-away space station for my eighth grade science project.

What a great idea. We made a papier-mâché donut, a torus. It didn't look half bad. I built all of the rooms: the control room, communications room, galley, sleeping quarters, etc. So the cut-away space station was born.

We made a backdrop, with stars and the earth's horizon. Dad helped me with the base and we mounted the space station onto a motor. We plugged it in; it worked.

When we took it to school it was a hit. I got an A and my teacher, Mr. Meade, convinced me to enter my space station project in the upcoming Buhl Planetarium Science Fair in Pittsburgh. This was a huge gala and there were all kinds of science projects and eggheads from all over western Pennsylvania.

The Buhl Planetarium was a pretty cool place. It had the old-style marble floors, pillars, and dark rooms to show off back-lighted pictures of galaxies. But the most memorable feature was the static electricity generator. Pittsburgh was the location of Westinghouse and General Electric. And these companies, I'm sure, put a lot of money back into the city. The static electricity generator was one of the many things they donated and was something I remember seeing when I was quite small, maybe five years old. Granddaddy took me there. There was a large, shiny gold ball that rose up from a pedestal. A hum or a faint buzz enveloped the entire room. The hairs on my body stood up. Suddenly a huge electric arc leapt from the ball to the ceiling with a horrific, deafening sound. I tried to cover my ears but Granddaddy pulled my hands down. It was so loud and so terrifying to me. Even in junior high school I didn't want to go to those "shows" because it brought back memories of incredible fear.

My space station won an award and my parents, Mr. Meade, and I went to the planetarium one evening for the award ceremony. I collected my ribbon and a prize: twenty-five silver dollars. That was a lot of money. I saved them for our second trip to Florida, which was upcoming.

Mr. Meade was a black man and I truly admired him. I knew my parents were very uncomfortable picking him up at his house in the black neighborhood. He was a gentleman and he radiated competency but with gentleness; it was infectious. My parents never fully relaxed but I saw that Mr. Meade was a terrific man and I learned so much on so many different levels from this one brief encounter outside of school.

10

Airplane and space books, science and plastic models—that was my life. I did manage to fit in things like baseball, football, and tennis but I was certainly nothing approaching a jock; far from it. I played tennis many times during the summer at the YMCA tennis courts behind our backyard. "The Courts," as we called them, became our hangout, and several of us endured our school life there in the evenings away from homework and parents.

Another spot I frequented was across our neighborhood. It was on a street that bordered the edge of a steep drop-off that overlooked the J&L steel mill. At night I would walk to this spot and sit on the guard rail, which was just a large cable strung between wooden posts, gazing down at the huge J&L plant hundreds of feet below. I called the spot "the wire" since "cable" didn't seem quite right to me. I spent many evenings at the wire throughout my school career. I thought about where I would be in five or ten years and it was there I pondered life in general. Later in high school I smoked cigarettes and spent more and more time at the wire struggling with adolescence issues.

I was invited by my Aunt Jean's brother, Bill, to go to the Pittsburgh Air National Guard. He flew jets there as part of his Air National Guard duty. I got to sit in the cockpit of an F-102A Delta Dagger jet interceptor. I started feeling the dream again, but quickly reminded myself of reality—the eye thing.

I was thrilled though and my boyhood urge came out again; I wanted to build another simulator. I liked to build things. But it would be something a little better than the one made out of Mom's old bureau. I was planning this project in the attic when Mother came up to get a box.

She casually said, "Ya know, don't you think you've outgrown this?

Why don't you think about rockets? Besides, rockets could open doors for you."

I was already very interested in rockets since I couldn't fly and the Space Race was in the minds of most at that time. That was a pivotal day; good ol' Mom had planted the seed that would grow and eventually get me out of my denial about my eyes and help me change my course.

Author in junior high school; 1964

Yes, I was your stereotypical egghead with the black horn-rimmed glasses. But this was a difficult time for me trying to deal with the social consequences of my wacko eyes, parent conflicts, and feeling pretty low in general over my dashed dream of flying jets. I hated to admit to myself that my mother was right. After more soul searching at the "wire," I concluded that if I couldn't fly, then I was determined to become a *real* rocket scientist. I pictured myself at one of those consoles saying, "GO!" I imagined working in the space program, and sometimes regretted not being born about fifteen or twenty years earlier so I could have been a part of the early rocket test programs or Project Mercury.

I saw the movie *I Aim at the Stars*, a sort of biography of Wernher von Braun and depiction of launching our first satellite, Explorer I, from a Jupiter C rocket from Cape Canaveral. I felt the excitement. I finally accepted a new goal. So it came to pass that I changed my Mike Mars plan, in my head anyway, to becoming one of the console guys in the space program. I wanted to launch rockets and satellites. But I still loved airplanes.

* * *

I saw an ad somewhere and ordered my first model rocket kit and rocket motors from Estes Industries in Colorado. These were already manufactured rocket motors. They were made with real rocket propellant but they were loaded into paper—thick paper—casings. After several days the package finally arrived; it was an Estes Industries Astron Scout. It stood an impressive four inches high. Also in the order were Estes rocket motors. Real rocket motors.

But my dream at that point was to build larger rockets and elicit others to join me. So I formed a club, the Aliquippa Rocket Club: me, Finney, Kent Sargent, and another neighbor and friend, Jerry Martin. My dad went with us up to the Flats. There weren't many flat places in the Appalachian foothills. But the top of the hill where we lived had been built up and leveled off many years before. The Jones & Laughlin Steel Corporation thought of building some sort of a rolling or finishing mill up there and brought up truck load after truck load of rocks and dirt and made a flat surface on which they were to build this plant. But it never panned out and J&L abandoned the site. It was a huge flat surface; hence the name the Flats, and it was perfect for kids.

It was there we launched the Astron Scout. It soared to about two hundred feet, then tumbled down. What a thrill. My first rocket launch April 4, 1964. I wrote everything down; see, good rocket scientists *do* that. So I wrote down the date and time of launch, name of the rocket, engine type, weather conditions, purpose of the flight, results, and any notes about lessons learned. Later on as an adult engineer, I would find that this practice gave me a good start properly preparing test plans and documenting the results in test reports. I took photos too. I noticed after I got them developed that Dad was watching from about three hundred feet away. He remembered the Science Club picnic and wanted no part of this four-inch-tall cardboard missile.

The next week, April 11, 1964, I launched no less than five rockets. I had purchased a "Designer's Special" that had a bunch of body tubes, nose cones, and fin material so I could make my own designs; after all, I was destined to become a rocket scientist. On this launch I invited my school class to climb the hill and watch the launch. About ten showed up, mostly girls, including Emily, my girlfriend from church. Yes, I had a few girlfriends, not many but I kept in touch with the real world of school, kids, and girls. Some girls liked guys with black-rimmed glasses and wacko eyes; who knew?

Dad borrowed a portable public address system from the mill and a newspaper reporter from the *Beaver County Times* showed up. This was big-time serious rocket stuff; and now… press conferences!

We had two more rockets to launch. The last rocket to be fired had a payload section that was, well, empty. I suggested putting a bug in it. We couldn't find a bug anywhere. We turned over rocks, nothing; looked in bushes, nothing. Where's a bug when you need one? They must have heard us and scattered. Finally, one of the club's staunch members, Jerry, said, "I know where to find a bug. I'll be right back." And off he went on his bicycle.

We prepped and then launched the next to last rocket and it floated down gracefully on its parachute. Then we saw Jerry with a jar in one hand and steering his bicycle with the other.

"What did you find?" Finney asked.

"A cockroach from our kitchen," Jerry replied with a little giggle. His small frame shadowed the rocket as he stooped down and gently nursed the cockroach with his hand into the nose cone; a few minutes later we launched it. The newspaper reporter interviewed me. I told him of the cockroach. I thought this was serious stuff. I mean we just did a rocket test on a bug. Years later I realized that he was almost crying trying to hold back the laughter.

HEADLINE, *Beaver County Times*, April 14, 1964: "Aliquippa Students Launch and Recover Bug Capsule"… "Dye said it was a little dizzy but otherwise unharmed by the rocket flight." He listed the names of the other conspirators too. We were famous. Watch out Wernher.

I experimented with different designs and got experience with rocket aerodynamics, at least the low-speed stuff since model rockets were only subsonic at that time. The rockets started getting larger as did the size of the motors I ordered. Then I clustered them; that is, we lit off about three or four rocket motors at the same time by clustering them at the base of a single rocket. The trick was to get them all to light at once. If one lit early, as the rocket lifted off, it could pull out the igniters of some, if not all, of the other unlit motors. An under-powered rocket would verrrrry slowly lift off, go up the three-foot launch (guide) rod, then keel over and fly in any direction.

How high did they go? one might ask. I asked that too. I wanted to be able to calculate how high it was going to go and then measure it. Estes Industries published a technical report that described how to calculate how high a rocket would fly. It was quite involved and required lots of calculations.

Mr. Abbott, who went to our church, was an engineer and the father of my girlfriend, Emily. He gave me one of his old slide rules and taught me how to do simple multiplication and division. I was in heaven. I was using a tool that just might lead me to the next step in my plan to be a rocket engineer.

I did do the rocket calculations using the slide rule—once. Even with the slide rule, it was laborious and I never did it again by hand; where's a computer when you need one? (That wouldn't happen for several years.) But I had a head start on mastering the slide rule in college later.

* * *

The next year, high school, I met some ham radio guys. They heard about the Rocket Club and contacted me, asking if they could provide a radio transmitter for the payload and monitor it during flight.

While this seemed pretty nerdy, let me assure you, it truly was. I was elected president of my own club (surprise), and others in the club started building rockets, even my neighbor and friend Finney. The only Chinese person I knew at the time was Pau Kee Fong. His parents ran the laundry and dry cleaner's at the end of Franklin Avenue. Pau Kee was an avid amateur photographer; he joined our club and enjoyed taking and developing photos of our rockets. We relished his photos, which he developed himself.

We had several launches. Each started on a Saturday at 6:00 a.m. when the winds were calm. We planned to make theodolites, a simple version of a surveyor's transit, to track the rockets to measure the maximum altitude. The trackers would be nearly five hundred feet from the launching pad and about one thousand feet apart, so we needed a communication system to connect with the guys doing the tracking. I checked out walkie-talkies, which seemed the easiest way to go, but with walkie-talkies, if someone is transmitting, no one else can transmit. So if the launch conductor was counting down from ten, no one could call a "hold" if something went wrong. They didn't work like telephones where you can hear and talk at the same time. So I suggested we go with telephones and everyone agreed.

My uncle Ed, who worked at Ma Bell, gave us old headsets that Mark DiVecchio, one of the ham radio guys, hooked up and they worked great. Dad was impressed that I didn't make a snap decision and he thought I led the club to the right choice.

The equipment for the rockets, the console, the firing system, the launching pads, the tracking theodolites, the communications system, and the transport vehicles to move all of this stuff made me, later, appreciate the ground support equipment (GSE) necessary to launch a rocket or test a satellite.

It also helped me with judgment over simple vs. complex, and when one needed each. "Keep it simple" started here, for me, with model rockets. Complexity spells disaster; simplicity in design and hardware equals success. I also learned that one should, to the greatest extent possible and within reason *and* without turning something simple into a science project, evaluate as many options as possible—but make a decision.

Decisions are a snap when we have 100 percent of the data. When we don't have all the facts, which we rarely do, we must also rely on experience, intuition, and, frankly, common sense when making decisions; furthermore, to the greatest extent possible, it's wise to seek recommendations from others. We don't have to take their advice but sometimes someone has an option, a thought or an idea that we haven't considered. This was the foundation of my professional career and it certainly paved the way to becoming a spacecraft manager many years later.

We started small but after a year or so we were launching rockets carrying radio transmitters in their payload sections (the nose cone).

The *Beaver County Times* was kind enough to print stories about us, advertising, at our request, that we were looking for members; no one showed up. Once they printed a full-page spread of photos from one of our launches at the Aliquippa Airport. We had a ball and, of course, the rocket failures were the most notorious.

My parents would accompany us to the launches. Turns out they were the only parents that volunteered to supervise us. They brought lawn chairs and would sit in the shade watching. Once, we counted down a cluster/radio transmitter rocket that had three motors to light at the same time. At ignition, one motor didn't fire. The rocket went up the rail, tipped over, and streaked right for their chairs. We were taking cover. My mother nonchalantly lifted her left leg as the rocket stuck in the dirt right under her chair! She just giggled and said, "Back to the drawing board, boys!" Unfortunately, she had occasion to say that way too often.

II

The rockets got larger and we had project planning meetings. After a few years we decided we wanted to "go amateur" and make our own rocket motors. To do this required metal parts, propellant, launch platforms, and static test stands; that meant money, and a lot of luck.

Bernie Carifo, one of the ham radio guys I had met earlier, was a rocket enthusiast as well, and we became very good friends. He had a '56 bright red Chevy wagon he called "The Apple." He and his dad would be flagged by police officers to follow fire engines to fires because they thought he was the fire marshal in his red wagon.

We used the wagon to collect scrap metal from anywhere we could find it and we did fairly well. We used the money from our Bill & Bern scrap metal cartel to finance rocket test stands and rocket motor production.

This was amateur rocketry. Until now, we were flying model rockets. Amateur rocketry was where you mixed your own propellants and loaded propellant into metal rockets, much like the high school Science Club adviser who mixed zinc and sulfur when I was in grade school. The good side is that you could make rockets that went up tens of thousands of feet. The bad side was that they frequently exploded while you were making them, either killing you or blowing off hands, eyes, whatever.

We wanted to do this right and, hopefully, not blow ourselves up in the process. We needed more information, so Bernie and I took the bus to Pittsburgh and then a streetcar to the Carnegie Library; there we read about and took copious notes on rockets. (This was before copy machines.) We found complete plans to build a zinc and sulfur rocket.

For a few months Bernie and I were testing fuel combinations in my basement, and we were becoming more and more knowledgeable about rocket propulsion and propellant chemistry.

One Saturday night, sometime in October 1966, my parents invited ten people over for bridge. Bernie arrived before the bridge party began, and before we descended into the basement I noticed that there were three or four card tables, coffee pots, and booze all waiting for the players. In the basement we worked for hours trying different fuel ratios and taking detailed notes. We made very small rocket motors by refilling old Estes rocket motor cases with our own propellant. We called them mini-motors and they were quite safe.

Test number ZS-44, all very scientific mind you, was burning and sputtered a bit. Some of the exhaust products, a hunk of burning propellant, from one of the mini rockets touched off a large beaker full of rocket propellant. Thick, white smoke billowed out of the vessel; then the beaker shattered. Glass and burning propellant were everywhere. Lots o' smoke now! We could see smoke going up through the floorboards, right into the living and dining room above. "OH, SHIT!" we both exclaimed about the same time. I could see the *Beaver County Times* headline: Rocket Boys Kill Bridge Party in Fire.

Actually there wasn't much of a fire, at least not after we put out the ping-pong table that was under the beaker, a towel next to the washing machine, our notes, and a half pack of cigarettes. With the fire out, we opened the cellar windows and tried to fan the smoke out. Hmmmm, we needed Plan B. Diversion was our only recourse. We propped the windows open and went upstairs with smoke and the stench of burnt sulfur clinging to our clothes. Trying not to cough, we nonchalantly walked into the living room where we saw streams of smoke coming up through the floorboards into an already smoke-filled room.

One man, my dad's boss, asked, "So what are you boys doing down there?" never taking his eyes off of his cards. I froze. Bern very professionally said, "We were attempting to increase the specific impulse of the propellant using thermite as a catalyst. The test was successful but it produced a little smoke."

They all nodded and murmured things like, "gooood" or "OOOOooo K", then, "three hearts," never taking their eyes from their cards. Bridge has got to be close to golf.

We went back downstairs to be sure nothing had re-ignited. The smoke was clearing and we calmed down a bit after the near catastrophe; our hands and eyes were intact. "Ruby Tuesday" by the Rolling Stones was on the radio. I now associate that song with bridge, Bernie, and burning zinc and sulfur.

A few weeks later we thought we had the best zinc and sulfur formula so we made a larger batch and loaded a rocket motor about ten inches long and an inch and a quarter in diameter and headed up to the Flats. We made the nozzle out of a material they used in blast furnaces, Castolast. A machinist made a metal mold for us so we could form the Castolast nozzle right in the rocket motor tube.

Earlier Bernie and I had built a large "blockhouse" out of thick plywood in his garage. This was for our future amateur rocket flights and we made it to fit perfectly inside the Apple. Now we were ready for some serious rocket testing.

But our zinc and sulfur rocket motors never worked very well—more flares, again, just like the Science Club picnic in grade school. So we went back to good ol' gunpowder. Up to the Flats we went with our battery, wire, and igniter. But this time we made a test stand with a spring/pencil assembly that measured maximum thrust. The rocket was strapped onto the stand and we strung the cable back to the blockhouse, which had a control panel with a Safe/Arm circuit to prevent accidental firings.

When all was ready we gave the traditional countdown and at zero hit the fire switch. A three-foot flame screamed from the nozzle for one second and then BLAM! The test stand (made out of plywood) was gone and there was a *crater* about three feet in diameter and about three inches deep! The little piece of paper that recorded the thrust was about all that was left: "Maximum thrust – 250 lbs." Over the next few weeks we did this about three or four times with the same result.

Bernie and I went back to the Carnegie Library and found after a little more research that our problem was heat transfer. We would much later appreciate the "it's not rocket science" expression when it came to experiments. But then we discovered liquids.

That same school year, 1966 to 1967, Bernie and I were seniors in high school and we told our chemistry teacher, Mr. Sampy, that we were experimenting with solid propellant rockets. "So, why are you guys messing around with solid propellants?" he asked. Now, mind you, this guy was the stereotypical chemistry teacher. He had the black horned-rimmed glasses and wore white socks—the true sign of the egghead in the sixties. We donned the black-rimmed glasses (this was before stylish glasses) but not the white socks. Didn't matter; we were just like Mr. Sampy.

He took us back to the chemical storage closet, a walk-in complete with wooden shelves, many stained with a collection of chemical spill stories. He selected a bottle of nitric acid, 98 percent molar solution, sort of like 98 proof, and furfuryl alcohol, pure. With resolve he pulled one large and one small glass beaker from another vintage wooden shelf and took these items back into the classroom to the "hood." The hood is an enclosure that protects the chemist from dangerous chemical vapors by sucking them up a stack and dumping them into the air to kill birds, trees, ozone, or whatever.

He put the beakers in the hood and filled the large one with about a half cup of red fuming nitric acid and the other with the same amount of alcohol. Donning an oven mitt he picked up the small beaker with a pair of tongs, lowered the hood to just over his wrist, turned toward us, and said with a smile, "Watch this!" Mr. Sampy dumped the contents of the small beaker into the larger one and quickly removed his protected hand and closed the hood...nothing.

Then, a second later, an ominous, thick reddish-brown cloud formed getting thicker and thicker, flowing over the edge of the large beaker like brown dry ice vapor. I felt myself moving back a few steps. He again turned and said, "Impurities burning off." Suddenly a bright flash and a *huge* flame streaked up the hood. The roar was incredible. The beaker shattered and a blinding fire ball engulfed the chamber but was quickly sucked away. As the smoke cleared, he looked at us and said, "Now *that's* rocket propellant! That's what we call hypergolic propellants; they ignite on contact."

"Cool."

We studied more about liquid rockets, sold more scrap metal to junk yards to get money for rocket parts. We tried so hard to build a liquid-fueled rocket, but college, girls (albeit few, for me anyway), in short, a life came upon us, and it all ended for a little while.

Preparing for the Space Program

12

The University of Pittsburgh accepted me but as a baby boomer with 60 million kids trying to get into college I had to go to the Johnstown, Pennsylvania, extension campus.

I filled out the forms and was notified that I had to go to Johnstown in August with the other freshmen for a few days as a pre-orientation meeting to meet my roommate and get tours of the new campus. New campus?

Pitt at Johnstown built a brand spanking new campus about five miles outside of Johnstown. The closest thing to the campus was a gas station a few miles away and a tiny strip mall three miles away. In other words it was out in the boonies.

I packed my suitcase and headed off, by bus, to Pittsburgh, walked across the city, and then took the Greyhound to Johnstown. It was the first time I'd been on a trip away from home by myself. I was anxious and excited at the same time.

The few days I spent there I met my future roommate, Nibs, and we got along great, and it was our introduction to the new University of Pittsburgh at Johnstown campus. We would be the first freshmen class to go there.

When I got home I could tell that there was a change in my dad.

Finally he mentioned something about me going to Johnstown alone and how this was a big step for me. Frankly, I thought so too. I was beginning to feel less reliant on my parents. The learning to be on my own process had begun.

* * *

At Pitt–Johnstown I planned to study aerospace engineering, although I was signed up for mechanical engineering with an aerospace option. Let's just say that it didn't go very well for me there. Partially because of poor study habits, and the more I feared failing the more I failed. It may also have been due to the fact that the school was trying to build their engineering reputation by flunking out 80 percent of the class. Out of a class of around two hundred engineering freshmen, two made it to the main campus; the rest quit, flunked out, or joined the army. The two who did go on made it with a 2.2 GPA—the highest in the whole class!

Dad was transferred from Jones & Laughlin Steel in Aliquippa to another J&L plant in Hammond, Indiana, and I decided to drop out of Pitt before they flunked me out. In January '69 I helped my mother sell our house in Aliquippa, and we packed the car, the cat and, you guessed it, peanut butter cookies, just like our Florida trips; I had two. Before we left the house we went into the attic and worked our way down to be sure we hadn't forgotten anything and also to say good-bye to the house that had been our home for at least thirteen years—most of my childhood.

In the attic I knew there was an almost empty pack of cigarettes hidden beneath one of the floorboards, and I reminisced in my mind about my jet simulator that I built there. I noticed the hole in the window sash where the cable from my wind vane and wind speed indicator was routed. The attic walls still had tack holes where I had photos of airplanes.

On the second floor I gazed into my bedroom with the peg board still in place but no models. Those got tossed along with my two shoe boxes full of baseball cards!

We finally ended up in the basement and we both stopped and stared at the wooden pillar beneath the stairs. It was painted white many years ago and on it were lines a lot closer to the floor with names next to them. The lines were the heights of Daniel DeSantis, Kent Sargent, Arthur Muskovich, Billy Dye, Buddy Nance, Phillip Brown, and a few others that we marked when we were all in Cub Scouts. We both started to tear up. Mom cried when I reminded her of our first Cub Scout meeting. We kept the kitty litter tray below the steps. Art Muscovich began to play in the sand, not knowing what it was for. In the middle of the meeting he interrupted my mom, held up a dried-out kitty turd, and said, "Hey, what's this?" Kent and Daniel did a "EWWwwww" and we all laughed, including Art.

On our way out I closed and locked the door noticing the crank doorbell. We walked down the porch steps and I stopped to look at the maple tree. I felt the warmth of summer heat and imagined the large leaves, remembering that day when I brought home the model of the B-36. But the tree was bare with remnants of snow around the base. The warmth and sunlight of that day I could only feel in my mind. It was our house, it was my life, and it was all to change. I felt incredible sadness as well as anxiety about my future.

We arrived in Munster, Indiana, about eight hours later and I helped them settle into their new home. I was 1A with the draft and I was in dire need of finding a school, but I figured with my eyes so out of whack I wouldn't be a good candidate for the army anyway.

Our new neighbor told us about an aeronautical school near St. Louis; they were on a trimester system meaning I could start school in April. That way I could get a student deferment for I would have certainly been drafted before that September.

I called the school and a nice lady said to please come down for an interview and a tour. I drove Dad to work, traveled the four to five hours down there, and spent considerable time touring the campus and the dorms. It's a school totally dedicated to aeronautics and aerospace. This was for me.

I started at Parks College of Aeronautical Technology, part of St. Louis University, in April 1969; I absolutely loved it. I enrolled in the aerospace engineering curriculum. They also had Aircraft and Power Plant (A&P), Airport Management, and associate aerospace degrees. Everyone there was interested in airplanes. Many flew airplanes and Parks had an airfield just off of the campus. Both the airfield and the campus were located in Cahokia, Illinois, just across the river from St. Louis. I was in the dorm, Mercury Hall, and it was just fine.

The school was basically all male; however, later there would be a few girls attending and by now I'm sure it's close to being coed. I hit the books hard right off the bat. My grade point average the first trimester was about 3.4. Wow! What a difference.

It had been a few months since I'd been home and I thought I would go home for the weekend and see my parents. My roommate offered to ride me to the train station in Chicago, where I could then take a Lake Shore train to Hammond. I agreed and plans were made. About a day before we were going to leave, he sheepishly told me that he and his girlfriend had set me up on a blind date for when we arrived at the Chicago suburbs. I was less than thrilled but decided to go through with it since I didn't have much choice at that point.

We piled into the car early that Friday afternoon and were in the suburbs of Chicago by five o'clock. We got out of the car to pick up the girls, and I saw this very nice-looking girl with long brown hair. But when she looked at me she laughed...going well so far. Apparently her friend, Linda, over sold me just a little, so I wasn't the Paul Newman-type she'd been expecting. Yeah, right, me with an eye out of whack, black horn-rimmed glasses, and long hair; definitely not a Paul look-alike.

She finally came up to me and we were introduced with not much eye contact, no pun intended. I was pretty ticked off. Her name was Joyce Dooley. She and I sat in the back seat of the car, opposite sides, as we headed for Chicago to put me on the train. Not too soon if you asked me. After a while Joyce and I were talking small talk and it was, well, OK. I mean she was pretty. Well, OK, she was really pretty.

They put me on the train and I spent the weekend with my parents and watched TV with Dad sharing a few bourbons and tobacco products. We'd start laughing and as our language started going south Mother would come out and say, "You guys are talking 'mill talk' again!"

Two weeks later the guys set me up again; same drill taking the train from Chicago. It was Joyce again. What gives? I guess she decided to give the wacky-eyed guy another shot. This time we really had a pretty good time. We laughed and she liked my sense of humor. She told me her birthday was in a week or so, on Bastille Day. I sent her a card: twenty-five points.

So there are two things I remember most about July 1969: First, I met Joyce and sent her a birthday card, and second, Neil Armstrong landed on the moon. In that order.

But the media coverage was intense—for Neil Armstrong, not Joyce's birthday. Days before the liftoff, the news coverage started and it didn't end until a few days after they got back. Walter Cronkite; he was the man. I watched him while he announced Alan Shepard's first flight on the Redstone, John Glenn's Mercury "Friendship 7" mission, countless Gemini and Apollo docking and checkout missions, and now the big one, the mission to put men on the moon. I watched him on TV in the Parks College commissary eating my orange peanut butter crackers and Coke. I was poor.

The landing on the moon was going to be one of those "where were you when" events. I marveled at the accomplishment but I have to admit that while in high school I feared that we wouldn't get to the moon, let alone beat the Russians. The Apollo fire and other seemingly unrecoverable setbacks disappointed me. But they did it and it was NASA's finest hour. I am truly grateful that I lived to see not only the moon landing but the entire manned space program from the start. What a thrill!

* * *

Since Parks ran on a trimester system we only got one month off, August, and that was it. Two weeks out of that August of '69 I spent at my roommate, Tom's, house; he lived in the Chicago suburbs near Joyce. I had a great time, spent a lot of time with Joyce, and it was during this period that she and I fell madly in love.

Joyce and I spent the next few years communicating by pay phone twice a week and I would travel to see her occasionally. The first year I visited her at Loyola University in Chicago, where she went her freshman year. To me it was a dreary, depressing campus; 'course it was pretty rainy every time I was there.

Later Joyce transferred to the University of Iowa, where she went her second year majoring in English. I took the bus there. It left St. Louis at 10:30 p.m. and got to University of Iowa, Iowa City, at 9:30 the next morning. I did that several times. I was deeply in love, you know.

Back at Parks College I needed to call long distance to Iowa. I would start collecting quarters for the pay phone. I'd call Joyce every Wednesday and every Sunday. I lived for those calls.

Dad gave me twenty-five dollars a month since my money from working at the J&L steel mill the summer of '68 ran out. But that just wasn't cutting it. I had to start working in the cafeteria. I got up at O-dark thirty to don an apron and wash dishes for about $1.75 an hour. Even with that, I was still poor.

This being in love thing, albeit via a pay phone, caused a disinterest in dances at Parks, where they bussed in girls from other schools. So my social life was limited to going out and drinking beer at the local college pub with the guys on Saturday nights. But, in a way, it was a blessing. I could focus on the books and work toward my dream.

13

Friday nights were my research nights. Parks had a great technical library and Friday night was about the only time I could justify doing research rather than studying. I didn't do this every Friday, but many. I read NASA reports on rocket engine technology with humongous titles and nothing but calculus. I tried and tried to make sense of these reports searching for the answer to a simple question: How does one design a liquid fuel rocket engine? Simple question, not a simple answer ... because, it's rocket science.

I studied every rocket paper imaginable; nothing. Finally, one day I found a new book by George Sutton entitled *Rocket Propulsion Elements*. This book had it all: how to design the rocket engine, the pumps, the tanks, everything. I mastered it and then went back to the technical papers. They still looked like Greek to me.

One day during my senior year, I was in an Advanced Aircraft Structures class and someone asked the instructor about technical papers and why they were so difficult to read. Gee, it's not just me, I thought.

The instructor laughed and said, "In order to be able to read them, you first have to know how they write them." Frowns of confusion.

"Look," he said, "the first thing you do is pick a title that is a very long sentence and has every technical term in it you can think of, like: 'Viscous Effects of Hypersonic Flow over a Rigid Body with Induced Boundary Layer Transition at High Angles of Attack.'"

"The second thing is don't use common symbols for standard things like A for Area, L for length. No, use Greek symbols, like lambda for area, gamma for length, and phi with an asterisk (gives it character) for something else.

"Third, never, never use simple arithmetic. If a PhD wrote it, then only a PhD in math should be able to read it. So, if the Area of a rectangle is Length times Width, one would normally say Area, A= L x W. No, no, no; never do this. You must use the calculus equivalent, in this case: (don't forget, we changed the definitions) Gamma = integral (phi* delta lambda) + sigma… where sigma is a constant."

After that, I realized I wasn't alone and for many years I wasn't as intimidated by the math or the people who professed to know it.

* * *

While at Parks College I met some other guys who liked rockets. There was no rocket club but there were several guys that were interested so I started a club. I brought some of the equipment left over from my Aliquippa Rocket Club days—stored in my parents' garage, something about which they were not terribly enthusiastic. We had lots of members and lots of launches. It was a dream come true to have so many people interested in the same thing and not all being nerds or rocket geeks… Well, OK, most were.

I had a rocket with a large motor that was designed to burn for ten seconds and put out about one pound of thrust. I put it in a large rocket saying to myself, It'll be just fine. The field at Parks College where we launched these things was huge. It was bordered by the dorm (lots of windows), a freeway (lots of cars), woods (lots of trees), and a railroad track (lots of trains). A target rich environment!

The wind was uncomfortably high. The rocket was a short, stubby thing that used to be a lot longer, but on a previous experiment it augured in from about one thousand feet and became shorter in the process, quite a bit shorter. The only thing left was the tail section and about nine inches of body tube. So I put a nose cone on it, called it a rocket, and installed my long-burning motor. What could go wrong?

Five…four…three…two…one…ppppffffffsssssssssssssshhhhhhhhhh. It rose ever so slowly up the six-foot guide rod. When it reached the top of the rod it arced over to near horizontal, since it didn't have enough speed, and it nosed right into the strong wind gaining speed. The rocket streaked across the field climbing ever so slightly, seven feet above the grass, ten feet, then fifteen. I began counting the ten-second burn at liftoff… "One one thousand, two one thousand, three one thousand…"

It was really moving, halfway across the field and still going. Then I heard MMRRrrrrrr. MMRRrrrrrr. "Oh, God, a TRAIN!" someone yelled. "With TANK CARS!"

"Seven one thousand, eight one thousand."

"Holy shit," someone yelled. "You're gonna take out the train!"

"Nine one thousand, ten one thousand...burnout!" I cried.

Silence. The rocket, now with no power, streaked toward the tank cars in a gradual descent from its maximum altitude of about thirty feet with smoke streaming out of the exhaust. Then only moments later: THUMP! It stuck into the roadbed four feet from the track. The guy in the caboose was leaning over the back railing to see what the hell it was that nearly killed his train. We saw his gaze follow the smoldering rocket stuck in the bed. He stopped, peered to the end of the field, and then hid in the caboose, probably in fear of a second round.

Too much rocket stuff, not enough time studying, so I hit the books pretty hard and put model rockets on hold for a couple of years. I knew I wanted to get into rocket propulsion. I wanted to design, test, and launch rockets; to be a console guy, I had to study.

* * *

One of my first engineering courses at Parks College was Statics. This deals with forces on things that, obviously, don't move. Well, hopefully not; things like bridges and buildings. This is a fundamental engineering class and whether you are a civil engineer, mechanical, aerospace, whatever, you have to take this class. (Civil engineers build structures but we "reframed" this by saying that they built targets.)

The Statics class at Parks was taught by Dr. Lin. Yes, he was a Chinese guy and was known to be very strict. Unfortunately his English was less than stellar and he was quite difficult to understand, but this was a mandatory and pivotal class and we all had to heed his direction.

"OK, crass, wee now huv bar lotating lound assis in crockrize dilection. Meeesar Barne, define moment, prease."

"Ahhhh, not sure I understand the question. Would you please repeat it?"

"No, you frunk." And he scribbled something into a little black book he kept on the podium.

"Meeessar Dye, prease splain moment."

"Force times distance."

"Velly good, you pass."

One kid on the first day asked, "Excuse me, what is 'Lotate'? No sooner did his mouth close after saying that did he realize what he had just said.

"You not funny, you frunk!" said Dr. Lin.

This went on all trimester. He was an *excellent* instructor, tough but really good; we just had to get used to his accent. I think I got a B.

Then there were the classes involving things that moved. These would be dynamics classes. It's dynamic; it moves. There was the basic Dynamics class dealing with solid objects that moved, like a ball rolling down a ramp, rotating things, levers, pulleys, or a cannon ball's flight. I liked the cannon ball problems because it was the basis for calculating rocket trajectories. There was also a *Fluid* Dynamics class. Guess what moved in that class? Yes, water. *Gas* Dynamics, the movement of gases through a pipe, through a nozzle (as in rocket), or over a surface (like a wing) was another class we had to take. All of these courses required us to do many problems to understand the principles. Lots of math, lots of numbers, lots of slide rule time (still no calculators). Problems, problems, and more problems; engineering is all about solving problems. And these courses got tougher not easier as we continued through the curriculum.

And then there was Thermodynamics. This is the study of the relationship between pressure, volume, and temperature on (usually) gases. Throw an aerosol can into a fire—not a bright idea, by the way—and, let's see, volume stays the same, temperature is increasing. What else could change? How about pressure? Yes, pressure. BOOM! When you blow up a balloon, the temperature stays the same but the volume changes. It's a feature of thermodynamics. There is a relationship between the *change* of volume with the *change* of pressure and the *change* of temperature.

Our Thermodynamics instructor was from India. Nice guy; knew his stuff. He had a very pronounced accent too. He was showing us a mathematical derivation of the relationship between the pressure, temperature and volume for a particular case. Now, in mathematics anything that changes is usually denoted as a delta or "d" for short. So the change in temperature would be delta T or dT. The change

61

In volume would be delta V, dV, and pressure would be dP. So the three basic variables were pronounced dee-T, dee-V, and dee-P. He also had a very bad habit of covering the blackboard, so his Indian thermodynamics dissertation went like this:

"Aund so, class you hab deis equation: Dee-wee dee-wee over dee-wee dee-wee times de square root of dee-wee dee-wee times dee wee dee-wee to dee 0.8 power. You sub-stee-tute dee-wee dee-wee with dee-wee over dee-wee and you get dee-wee dee-wee. Do we hab any questions? No? Den hab a good day, class deismissed."

I think I got a C+ or a B. We loved the guy and we learned a lot from him.

14

I completed all of the basic engineering classes like Thermodynamics, Fluid Dynamics, and Gas Dynamics. The fun courses like Aerodynamics, Aircraft Structures, and others including one of my electives, Propulsion, started around the second or third trimester of my junior year at Parks College.

In Aerodynamics 101 we got to design our own airplane. The class took us through the design process and every week we got a new task. The first week we had to produce a three-view drawing of our airplane design and select an airfoil section. NACA, the old NASA, in the early years created a system that would describe the shape of airfoils or wing cross-sections. We had to choose one from a gigantic book.

The next class was to determine the lift and drag of the airplane, and the next to determine the service ceiling—or how high it would fly. Each week our Aerodynamics professor would pick a few of us to go to the head of the class and present our results, showing all the math we used to get our performance numbers.

We were nearing the end of the trimester and the crunch was on to complete all the remaining tasks in time for the last few classes. I was up all night with the slide rule doing calculations and I had everything completed except takeoff distance and landing distance. The equations for these were monsters. I looked at the clock: 7:30 a.m. The class was at 8:00. No way. What to do? I thought of something, marked up my drawing, and went to class. I figured with all of topics to be covered and the number of students, what were the odds of me being called, let alone for the topic I was least prepared for?

The class started. All of us had our three-ring binders, our rolled up three-view airplane drawings, and our slide rules.

"Jeff, front and center, show us your time to climb calculations," the instructor barked. And Jeff came to the front of the room and went through his calculations.

One down.

"Bernard, front and center. Show us your max range calculations." Two down. My fingers crossed. "Dye."

Oh, God, please don't let it be takeoff and landing distance.

"Front and center. Show us your takeoff and landing distance calculations."

I didn't blink. I grabbed my three-view drawing, unrolled and tacked it to the narrow cork strip above the blackboard. I spoke as I wrote numbers on the blackboard. "The takeoff distance is one hundred and fifty feet." Everyone laughed.

"And the landing distance," I continued above the laughter, "is one hundred and twenty five feet." Uproarious laughter now.

The professor said, "Mr. Dye, do you really think an airplane can get off the ground within one hundred and fifty feet?"

"Why yes, sir, I do."

"So where are your calculations?"

"I didn't have to do them, sir," I said.

"Please explain."

I turned to my drawing. My design was a single-engine propeller fighter airplane. I pointed to the side view where I had written "NAVY" in big letters on the fuselage and said, "The takeoff distance is one hundred and fifty feet, the length of the aircraft carrier catapult. The landing distance is one hundred twenty-five feet, the distance to the second wire." Everyone howled. Fortunately so did Dr. Bondi. I didn't know the real distances. I guessed.

Ah yes, creativity; it worked. I got a laugh out of him as well as a B. Oh yeah, and the distances were just about right.

Now don't get me wrong. I wasn't a smart ass all through school; far from it. Anxiety and determination to "reach the dream" were with me all the time. I really didn't do well grade-wise in school because I froze at test time. I was so anxious about failing that I frequently did. I couldn't concentrate. But I certainly learned the principles.

Aerospace engineering was no cake walk. I still have the anxiety dreams like finding out halfway through the semester that you've missed all of the Advanced Physics classes because you forgot you had signed up for the class and the mid-term is tomorrow! You know these dreams. The classes at Parks got tougher each year and I never really mastered the art of studying; hence, my steadily decreasing grade performance. I still froze during exams, which really cramps your style if you have to do five complex engineering problems in a fifty-minute class period. But, in spite of my performance, I knew the material. Then there are those with a 4.0 average that don't know how to make or build anything or have no common sense and blindly believe the computer. Later, as a manager, I looked for people who used the course material to solve problems, not necessarily with math, although we needed that and them too, but more intuitively. I always asked them on interviews what they had done and had they ever built anything, either at school or as a hobby.

I may have done better in school if I had sought help. But I was so worried that I would be labeled as a suck-up if I went to see a professor to ask a question or to show me what to do. I think you could count on one hand the number of times I went to see a prof. That was a mistake. I also learned about power, abuse of power! I got a D in a philosophy course because the idiot professor stated that there have been absolutely no advances in technology due to war. I spoke up and asked him what he thought about nuclear power, missiles, little things like that. He called me a warmonger, and he graded me accordingly to punish me for contradicting him in class. My real failing was not confronting him privately. The lessons we learn.

I enjoyed labs though. I found that I had an innate desire to tell a story with a test report. I always wanted any engineer to pick up a test report that I prepared and be able to understand exactly what I did, what equipment and settings I used, and easily understand the data as presented and the results. This paid off later in my aerospace career.

Mother and Dad came down to see me once or twice. They were thrilled that I was *passing* and not struggling as I did at Pitt. We went to Trader Vic's once in downtown St. Louis and I bored them to death with things I learned and people that I met. My dad's constant smile spelled relief that I was "making it." But sometimes I felt my mother's envy. She never wanted to be a housewife. Sometimes Patty and I believed she never wanted children since she told us countless times about experiences when she was working. She wanted to be closer to airplanes too. But she was thrilled for me to be capturing my dream and, in a way, hers.

15

At the beginning of my Parks College senior year I approached my propulsion professor with a proposition to build a liquid propellant rocket engine. I told him of my research and how I'd been studying rocket engine design and I wanted to give it a shot. The rocket engine was not going to be a flight model, but rather a "heavy weight" design that could be used as a tool for demonstrating rocket propulsion to future classes; a static test engine. I gave him my plans. The rocket engine was to be a 1,000-pound thrust engine using liquid oxygen and kerosene as propellants. He was intrigued and said he would approach the dean.

Two days later, he told me the dean said it was too big and would cost too much to build and maintain. OK, so it was big, but it just has to be, I thought. After a while, I realized that just as I had to make compromises in design, I also had to compromise in terms of what I wanted. I revised the plans and presented a 500-pound thrust rocket engine using gaseous oxygen and kerosene.

Still too big! OK, how about a 100-pound thrust? Still too big. I started thinking like Maxwell Smart on the 1960s *Get Smart* TV series. "Would you believe...100-pound thrust using liquid oxygen and methane?"

No.

"Would you believe 10-pound thrust, gaseous oxygen, and methane?"

YES!! Finally.

I began my modestly sized rocket project by approaching the guy who was the school machinist. He was a navy "chief" salty-dog type.

"You wanna build whuuut?" he grumbled as he looked at my plans, tattoo showing through his shop shirt, spittoon on the floor. Memories of the steel mill suddenly came back; another story. Then he muttered something that I would hear frequently in the next few years, something about "these damn college kids," mumble, mumble.

He scribbled on the drawing pointing out how the drawing should have been dimensioned so that it would make sense to a machinist. That was Professional Lesson No. 1: The people who *make* the stuff are the best source for helping you *design* the stuff so it can be built.

After I'd made some drawing changes to his satisfaction, he made the combustion chamber and a water-cooling jacket that slipped around the engine and provided a means to flow water around the chamber during a firing to keep it from melting.

I had all the parts except one. I got "K" bottles of compressed gases for the propellants. All I needed were regulators to control the flow of gases. None. They had to be ordered and it was only a few weeks before I graduated, so, alas, I never got to see the rocket engine fire. About six months after I graduated, I got a letter from the professor, Dr. Black. He said they hooked it up and fired it and it worked! "It made one hell of a noise!" he said. (Still too big.)

* * *

Finally, graduation. Dad was gleaming! He was *so* proud of me. And this pleased me. My mother was so excited I thought she would burst. I had an aerospace engineering degree. I'd made it. I was on my way.

I was disappointed though that in July 1971 there were no aerospace jobs, certainly none with my rather average GPA. This was the time of the century when PhDs in aerospace were pumping gas. The Apollo program was winding down; no new bombers; no new fighters; the supersonic transport passenger jet, the SST, died because we were afraid the sonic boom would kill fish. So the Brits and French built the Concorde and just look at the tons and tons of dead fish spanning the ocean. Now, mind you, I am actually fond of our environment, I do care, but sometimes any group or organization behaves irrationally, like prophecies of fish dying from sonic booms. I'm more concerned about the pollution of our oceans—way more impact than a sonic boom—but no one protests cargo ships.

Parks College was great and I was thankful for my degree but I was sick of tests, papers, anxiety, and textbook problems… and did I mention anxiety? I didn't even look back as the car pulled away. I wanted to climb the next rung on the ladder of reaching my dream. I wanted the next step, the *big* step. I wanted into the space program.

16

It was July 1971 when I graduated from Parks College with a B.S. degree in aerospace engineering. As soon as the Draft Board realized we students were graduating, they drafted us. I was no exception and I was sent a letter requesting me to take a physical for induction into the Armed Services. But with my crooked eyes I failed the physical and, hence, was not drafted nor destined for Vietnam, as I had expected. My army physical, however, had to be one of the funniest experiences of my life. Thirty guys walking around in their underpants carrying little paper bags with their valuables.

About four months after I graduated, and over one hundred fifty mailed resumes later, I found myself working in a lumber yard near Hammond, Indiana, for $2.50 an hour. It was November 1971 and I was putting price tags on Christmas ornaments in an unheated warehouse, sitting on a stool replete with a piece of cardboard beneath it to insulate me from the cold concrete floor. I was thrilled to death.

After a month or so I quit tagging ornaments and got a job with a company that had a heated building. I was hired by the Simmons Corporation Mattress Testing Center as a mattress specifications writer. This was great. At parties it was fun to tell people what I did for a living—mattress tester! The Simmons people were very nice to me. They gave me a week's vacation after being there only a few months so we could go on a honeymoon. Yes, Joyce and I were married on April 22, 1972. It was a small wedding.

On our wedding day Bob Schneider ("Schneidly"), my best man, some other friends I made through school, and Joyce, my sister Patty, her husband Larry and their two-year-old daughter Kimi sat around the piano bar singing and drinking; all except Kimi, that is. Later that evening we had a terrific send-off to Florida for our honeymoon. Florida was the only place in the States that was warm in April and that we could afford. Plus, I'd been there so at least I knew what to expect—cuts down on anxiety. We liked it so much down there we stayed another two days. This wrecked havoc with the airline and ended up costing us a bunch of bucks to get home. But it was fun. Although Joyce is always embarrassed to tell people that we went to Treasure Island; that's just south of Tampa, and a lot of old people live in Tampa, you know.

The Simmons people were easy people to be around and to work with. About a month after I was hired, word got around that I was interviewed for my job by the plant manager. Apparently no one had been interviewed by him before. He interviewed me because he wanted to see what an aerospace engineer looked like. I bet *he* was surprised. Good thing *The Simpsons* wasn't on TV then: Homer – Aerospace Engineer. D'oh.

On December 7, 1972, the night Apollo 17 lifted off, I got a call from the manager of Wind Tunnel Operations for North American Rockwell with an offer to work on the Space Shuttle Program doing wind tunnel testing. Finally! When I got off the phone I screamed with joy! Joyce was excited too.

The day I left Simmons, the plant manager asked me, "Bill, why do you want to go to California? Aerospace will come and go but people will *always* sleep." He had a point, and there were times during my aerospace career when that thought came back to me. But I had to go. I had lived for this day.

The Simmons plant closed down a few years later.

So *This* is the Space Program

17

Joyce and I packed up our sparse belongings, acquired after only nine months of marriage, and moved from our one-bedroom apartment in Lansing, Illinois, to California. The weekend before we left I spent time with Mother and Dad. Again, Dad had that smile on his face that beamed with pride. He told me, as he had several times before in my life, "Boy, you're going to be a freshman all over again."

Mother was quiet. I could tell she was torn. We lived in Lansing, Illinois, only ten minutes from their house. Now we would be across the country. She was really looking at an empty nest now. But she shared the dream. If she were me she would go in a minute and not look back; and that's the feeling I got from her.

A few days later, the moving van came. Joyce and I had the car packed and were ready to go. Dad came to our apartment from work around lunch-time to see us off. We didn't even know he was coming. I don't think he ever told Mother that he came to see us off.

As we drove away in our '72 Plymouth Duster I looked back and saw him standing there with his trench coat, pipe, and '50s-style hat—just like he did when he watched my first rocket flight only nine years earlier. He was smiling but I could sense his mixed emotions. He knew

71

Joyce and I were starting off on our life adventure together. We truly were freshmen again.

It took us several days to cross the country. Joyce had found out earlier that she was hypoglycemic and the only real cure was to enhance her diet with protein. All the way to California she made and drank a Brewer's yeast concoction. She did this for several months and it worked. It also showed her the path of eating healthy foods and visiting health food stores; this rubbed off on me too. Well, somewhat.

To get to California from Chicago in the first week of 1973, we decided to go south to avoid snow. It took a couple of days to cross Texas, New Mexico, Arizona, and finally we arrived at Downey, California, home of North American Rockwell, Space Division. The letter said, "Member, Technical Staff, Aerospace Flight Sciences Department." The salary was $878 a month; that beat $375 a month gross from Simmons.

Monday, first week of January 1973, my first day in aerospace and I didn't feel the least bit anxious. I was ecstatic! After three hours of completing personnel forms I was summoned by the group secretary, Pat, who was to escort me to my new job. Mini-skirts were very popular and ogle-eyed males had no idea that twenty-five years later one could be fired for, well, just looking. But Pat's short skirt was impossible to not notice. Any slight lean on her part and her underwear showed.

Pat and I arrived at the Wind Tunnel Operations Department in the mezzanine. I was to begin my work there as a wind tunnel test engineer testing the new space shuttle design. It was a long, narrow room with old wooden floors. There were groups of desks arranged in columns all facing one desk at the front; that desk was turned so that it faced the rows of desks. Just like school. The guy at the front desk was the supervisor. Between the supervisors was a low partition, less than three feet high. The next supervisor, same set up. This went on for quite a distance.

Our supervisor's name was Paul. He led our department, Wind Tunnel Operations, which had about twenty guys, so it was three columns of six or seven desks facing the supervisor. He had a rug below his desk. We had linoleum; old linoleum. We coveted our linoleum. We each had three and a half squares of linoleum that set the distance from the edge of the guy's desk behind you to the front edge of your desk. So three and a half linoleum squares is all the room you had for your chair; there were no cubicles, no plants, no book shelves, no filing cabinets, and certainly no windows.

The other very important factor was rank. The more senior you were, the closer you got to sit to "the front of the class." So that put me in the, ah...back. I found out later that the supervisor running the aerodynamics department next to us actually had something like a hall pass to leave the area. And some of those guys were PhDs. 'Course they were thinking, "Better than pumping gas."

I was introduced to my new coworkers. They were just regular guys. They didn't smoke pipes, didn't have calculations all over their desks, and didn't talk about current space missions. No, they were talking about their camping trips to Yosemite, Mammoth Lake, and Sequoia National Park.

They soon found out that I had never had Mexican food. Ben Herrera, a guy from Cuba who always called Tacos ("TACK-os"), took me to Estralita's Taco House on Bellflower Boulevard in Bellflower, next to Downey. The green chili burritos were so good, and hot that tears came to my eyes. After work, I told Joyce about this place, and for the next four and a half years we spent at least one evening of the weekend at Estralita's. OK, so we did healthy food six days a week.

Everyone wore either leisure suits—I never bought one—or polyester pants; I did buy those. The desks at work were real old wooden jobs. Antiques. The bottom edge of the center drawers were all worn, frayed, and splintered from years of people rubbing the bottom of the drawer with their thighs as they were sitting down or getting up. So combine a thirty-year-old splintered wooden desk and polyester pants... several times a day you'd hear someone yell, "DAMN IT! I just bought these pants." As I walked down the halls I would see guys with little foo-foo balls hanging from their crotch or thighs, snags from their desk drawers.

After being there about a month it was time to move. Apparently, the company made money by moving people around the facility. "Cost plus" contracts with NASA provided moving expenses, or so I was told. So I packed up all my stuff that Friday and labeled it for them to move it over the weekend; one box. Joyce picked me up—we had one car in those days—and we went to the drive-through bank and then to Estralita's.

Monday I found my way to my new building and entered through an old metal door. Inside there were all kinds of beams, rafters, lights, and ventilation ducts several stories up overhead, and birds. I had to be in an aviary. But I wasn't. I was in a large hangar. There were birds everywhere. What a racket! A week later Pat, showing off her pink underwear today, was giving out stickies that she pasted on our desks. There were stars for filling out our time cards correctly; arrows for when we successfully zapped a bird with a rubber band (confirmed by at least one other employee); and mushroom clouds for…well, if the bird won, which no one needed to confirm. Lots of stars, only a few arrows, but *plenty* of mushroom clouds adorned our desks. Each evening we would either "chance it" or put a piece of plastic over our precious papers. I usually chanced it because I didn't have many precious papers.

Computers were those big things with blinky lights in special rooms. The first calculators were just coming out. Seventy-five bucks for a four-function plus square root calculator. The negative sign was a little red light that lit up through a teeny hole, so you had to hold the calculator just right to see the light. Texas Instruments had a full engineering calculator for about 175 bucks; pass.

Some guy in the Aero Department hooked up a plotter to a small computer; it sat on a desk, had about 2K memory, if that. It made a graph. He was a hit. Even the manager came over to watch this machine make a plot.

The cups in the coffee machines had a four-card poker hand on them with the fifth card on the bottom of the cup. You had to raise the cup to see the bottom card, preferably without spilling coffee on your face. Once, Scott Crossfield was there. He drove the X-15 rocket plane. I just couldn't muster the courage to introduce myself to him since all I could think of saying was that I did my seventh grade science project on the X-15. And he would pat me on the head and say, "Gooood." So I just eavesdropped.

I heard him say, "It was a real kick in the pants," describing what it felt like when the X-15 exploded during a static engine test a few years earlier. The explosion shot the cockpit, with him in it, about thirty feet across the desert. He too had a poker coffee cup in his hand. I noticed him raise the cup to see the bottom just before he threw it away.

The scene indelibly burned into my mind is me sitting at my desk, calmly picking at the corner of one of my many "mushroom clouds," hearing the flapping of wings and chirping echoing through the huge hangar, and watching several guys standing at the coffee machine, all with little fuzzy foo-foo balls hanging from their crotches, holding up their brew looking at the bottoms of their cups. Ah, I thought, so *this* is the space program.

18

I was assigned to support tests in the Aerodynamic Heating section of our very small Wind Tunnel Operations Department. I would be testing models of the space shuttle for launch ascent as well as reentry heating to determine whether the vehicle would burn up during the launch or reentry. I was in model heaven. Oh, yeah, we were not allowed to use the term "reentry" until after the first flight. Some manager said that if it reentered, that meant it had entered once before and it hadn't. I still said reentry.

I got to test many different types and sizes of models in several NASA and Air Force wind tunnels. I did most of my testing with an OTS model (Orbiter + Tank + Solid rockets), the Orbiter model being about twenty-four to thirty inches long.

We were quite concerned about the tiles since they were to protect the Orbiter from the tremendous heat generated during reentry. We had to see if they would work and how precisely they would have to be installed. One type of wind tunnel test we did was called a phase-change paint test. We applied special white paint to a black model made from high temperature resistant epoxy. The white paint turns clear, or "changes phase," at a specific temperature. The model was photographed with motion picture cameras and a young engineer, that would be me, had to draw where the melt line was, move the film several frames, and draw another line and another until all the paint turned clear as I viewed it on a film table. Later we got rid of the paint and used infrared (IR) cameras; much easier.

Space Shuttle phase-change paint model in the NASA/Ames 3.5 foot hypersonic wind tunnel
Courtesy of NASA/Ames

Author with Orbiter phase-change paint model
Courtesy of NASA/Ames

Other models were built from stainless steel and were instrumented with hundreds of thermocouples that measured temperatures. The aerodynamic wind tunnel models used instruments inside the model to measure lift and drag, and flutter models simulated the physical properties of, say, the wing and were put into a wind tunnel to see if the wing fluttered. Some did and when they fluttered the wing would rip off; test over. I always thought those would be great tests to be on since you usually came home early!

Stainless steel thermocouple space shuttle model in the NASA/Ames 3.5 foot hypersonic wind tunnel
Courtesy of NASA/Ames

At the time, there were actually some supervisors and managers that were looking ahead to the first shuttle flight with respect to correlating flight data to wind tunnel data. The top surface of the wing had a different type of insulation than the tiles since the heating rates were significantly lower than the bottom of the wings, which took the brunt of the reentry heating. They wanted to be sure they had sufficient margin, so they called a meeting to discuss ideas for getting some actual flight data from the top surface of the Orbiter wing during the first reentry. This wasn't a safety issue. It was more: Can we use easier-to-maintain insulation to save maintenance costs and turnaround time?

I, the kid two years out of college, was actually invited to this meeting. I sat with the department manager, my supervisor, and the aerothermal analysis group supervisor. I was there because Paul thought they might modify one of my wind tunnel models to collect supplemental preflight data and I might shed some light on how difficult these modifications might be. There was a lot of discussion about ways to instrument the top surface of the real wing. Well, I went and opened my mouth and said, "Why don't you put an infrared camera in a pod on top of the vertical tail looking down on the top surfaces of the fuselage and the wings?"

Silence. Gee, they didn't laugh! They actually listened and discussed it for about ten minutes. But it didn't sound like they were going to do it. So to promote my great idea I said, "Well, you could also put a camera up there too. It would be great for public relations. Wow! A shot of the Orbiter during re...oops, sorry, entry."

Silence ...glares...mumbling. That did it. The manager stood up while he closed his tablet portfolio and said, "No pod with a camera and, Paul, talk to this kid about this, will ya?" More glares. Meeting over.

Yikes!

Paul pulled me into his office, the supervisor's desk with Astroturf, and said, "We never, ever, ever talk about doing something for 'PR.'"

"Why?" I asked.

"Because," he said, "several years ago we lost one of the XB-70s because of 'PR.'"

"Huh?" I said.

"General Electric made the engines for the XB-70. They asked the Air Force if they could get all the airplanes that GE supplied engines for and fly them around the XB-70 and get a group shot for a GE publicity photo shoot. So they flew the XB-70 with all of the other aircraft in the Air Force inventory that used the same engines to get this publicity photo. They flew a Lear jet next to the formation to film it and get the shots.

"They wanted a 'tight' formation for a better picture. An F-104 got too close, got caught in the wing tip vortices of the XB-70, and rolled across its back clipping off the vertical stabilizers. The XB-70, F-104, and another aircraft went down killing a few of the pilots. North American decreed they'd never do anything like that again."

"Oh…uh…I see."

* * *

After a few months we moved out of the hangar back into a "desk and board" area, i.e., an area not suitable for birds. This move was a little different, however. It was mid-week. We packed up as usual and were ready to go when the phone guys came in. They said they had to move the telephones too. One of my coworkers, Don, was talking on the phone, on business, and the phone guy says, "Hey, I gotta move this phone." Don gestured like "yeah, yeah" and three seconds later I heard Don tapping the receiver button and saying, "Hello? Hello?" The phone guy grabbed the phone out of his hands and said, "Hey, I told ya I need the phone," as he wrapped up the cord he had just yanked out of the wall.

* * *

Friday was cleaning day. Unlike many corporations and institutions, North American Rockwell decided it would be just fine to have the janitors work in occupied work areas during the day. They ran vacuums on the hall rugs and the supervisors' rugs. These vacuums put out a very loud high-pitched whine, like a whistle, an ear-piercing whistle. There we sat, about a dozen of us, and along came the janitor. We heard the slapping of the cord on the floor as he played it out and then plugged it in.

The vacuum started and one by one we all started whistling a constant tone that matched the exact pitch of the vacuum. The Guidance and Control guys next to us caught on and start whistling too. Before long, the place was rocking with this ear-splitting shriek. Our supervisor walked over to the vacuum to see why it made so much noise, so we slowly toned down the whistles as he neared the janitor. He scratched his head and walked away. As he got closer to his desk we all started whistling again. He put down his pencil and walked over to the janitor again and returned still baffled. We all had to keep our heads down because if anyone looked up we would all burst out laughing.

This went on for several weeks, every Friday. It was getting harder and harder to keep from laughing as the janitor prepared the vacuum each time. Then one day Paul, who turned out to be one of the best supervisors I ever had in my entire aerospace career, left the room before the janitor arrived. We started our ritual as the vacuum came to life. Suddenly we heard, "ALRIGHT, YOU GUYS!" He had circled around and sneaked up behind us. He couldn't contain himself and started laughing. Soon, day vacuuming ceased.

* * *

Staff meetings were also on Fridays from 2:30 to 3:30 p.m. Not us, only the managers and supervisors. We never went to meetings; they never told us anything; we didn't ask. Without the Friday janitorial service sing-along we became restless. We needed a challenge and for several weeks we had one. This new facility was in a huge bay, no partitions, with department after department just about as far as you could see. To our left was Guidance and Control; to their left was Public Relations (saw Walter Cronkite there once, which was more thrilling for me than seeing an astronaut!); to their left was Dynamics; to their left was Shuttle Integration. The "lefts" went on forever.

Friday, 2:25 p.m. All supervisors and managers started to clear out to attend the staff meeting. This would be about week five with "no joy." Anticipation grew. Drawers opened. Rulers, rubber bands, and paper clips were arranged on the tops of the desks. Discretion was still required; the meeting could be canceled or cut short. By now all of the managers were out of the room. When the conference room door closed, a hush came over our group, and then the next and the next until the entire enormous room was quiet. Waiting.

One man stood: Ellis Chee. He lifted his arm and held up a small yellow object that looked like a model airplane and loudly said, "OK, you guys, take your best shot," and he let go of the small "ornithopter," a rubber-band powered thing that loudly flapped its wings and propelled itself across the expanse. We missed birds.

It was thunderous and quick, clacking each time its wings flapped to propel it over the bays of engineers. Antiaircraft fire opened up and it was heavy. It flapped its way passed our Wind Tunnel Operations group. Rubber bands, paper clips, sling shots, blow guns made from straws, everything imaginable was in the air. It kept going. It passed Public Relations. All the streaks in the fluorescent sky could not touch the ornithopter. Would this be the sixth week with no one hitting the bird? It flapped its way past Thermal Analysis. *Ting, tang*: paper clips ricocheted off of the light fixtures. The sound of the flapping was almost drowned by the whizzing sounds of the projectiles.

But then, someone in Avionics had a secret weapon, a huge pretzel-shaped paper clip spread apart and pulled back on six rubber bands thumb-tacked to a wooden ruler. The clip was spread open to increase the size of the projectile. It launched. The sheer mass of the clip and its speed was no match for the ornithopter. The large speeding missile walloped the 'thopter. An explosion of yellow plastic flew everywhere. Its thunderous flapping sound was silenced. The entire room exploded in a massive cheer.

The tail landed in Guidance and Control and the wing-flapping mechanism made it to Aerodynamics. The 'thopter died a quick death. Suddenly the meeting room door opened and out came the managers and supervisors. The cheering stopped; ornithopter pieces still floated to the floor; another picture of innocence. One last rubber band fell from a light fixture onto a desk, *frap.*

19

Wind tunnel testing is one of the best jobs in aerospace because you get to work with the whole vehicle, but the travel requirements of the job were hard on marriages and social life, mine included. It was virtually impossible to have any sort of social life requiring date-setting or long-term planning; you just didn't know when you would be in town. As a newlywed, this was not an ideal situation.

Every day, I worked with three view drawings of the space shuttle and worked with the models a great deal of the time. I was like Fred McMurray on the *My Three Sons* TV series about an aerospace engineer in the early '60s.

As a wind tunnel test engineer, I was to deliver quality data, which meant a quality model and test. My task was to first prepare the requirements for the design of a wind tunnel model that would successfully collect the desired data—what wind tunnel, the model size, angles of testing in the wind tunnel, where the instruments should go, and how would they be routed to the facility panels. I had to insure that the model was designed properly, that all the details for integrating the model to the wind tunnel were planned out. I also had to supervise the shipment and installation of the model into the wind tunnel test section being sure that the instrumentation was hooked up properly. And then finally I had to conduct the test, verify the data quality, and write a test report.

Looking back on this, I used to feel a little "left out" since I didn't do the analytical work. But I later realized that as a test engineer I had to coordinate, negotiate, and direct. All of these people skills paid off later in my career. I very quickly learned about people, what makes them happy, what makes them productive, and most importantly I learned to treat people like I would want them to treat me. Aerospace is no different from any other job. It's a job, with good days and bad days. The trick for me, especially much later on, was to try to enjoy the people and the things we worked on and not focus on the hassles.

The space shuttle was quite a challenge. Then, in 1973-74, what was a perfect wing design for the aerodynamicists would burn up during reentry or it would survive reentry but wouldn't do for landing. Eventually, it would take several wing designs to get just the right design. When I joined the organization, they were on about the fifth wing design. And it had just changed again.

One day Paul barked, "Bill, go see George and get the new wing drawings. He's in the mezzanine."

"Who's he?" I asked.

"He's the shuttle designer."

I knew where the mezzanine was because we had worked there four moves before. When I arrived at the mezzanine, I saw a man sitting at a large drawing board; this was before computer automated drawing systems. He had an electric eraser in one hand and a drawing pencil in the other; cigarette ashes were everywhere. He had a little Clark Gable-type moustache and his hair matched the color of the dark coffee he was drinking. I introduced myself. He said his name and we shook hands. I asked him to repeat his last name.

"Owl, George Owl," he barked. I had just read a book about the XB-70, as I wanted to read up on my earlier "public relations" blunder. The book mentioned the XB-70 designer, George Owl. It was him! I had to be sure so I asked, "Are you *the* George Owl, the designer of the XB-70?"

"Yeah," he said. "So?"

There was no plaque, nothing; and this guy was *famous*. This was the man that designed one of the most beautiful flying machines ever built. And there was no one there but me. He saw the look on my face and said, "It's no big deal, kid," as he took a long drag on his filterless cigarette. But he had a look in his eye. Like he'd been hurt, but somehow not directly; as if there *should* have been a plaque, but there was none. Either that or it was at home on his mantle or in a cardboard box in his garage. Somehow I didn't think so.

No plaque, nothing, for designing the XB-70

Or maybe he was weary of young punk college kids. In any event, George and I were on a first-name basis after two minutes. I told him of my mission to find the new wing drawings and he gave me a copy of the freshly printed blue-line drawings of the shuttle. Blue-lines were prints made by an ammonia process that left blue lines on white paper. When you got fresh blue-lines they could clean out your sinuses about as well as a good slug of horseradish.

The piercing shot of ammonia from the printing process stabbed my sinuses as I unrolled the print. On the profile (side) view of the Orbiter I noticed an arrow pointing to the bottom of the nose of the vehicle. It said, "KE-008." I studied this along with the rest of the dimensions. I could figure everything out except KE-008. So being right out of school, filled with differential equations, calculus, and the like, I assumed this was the label for an equation that just *had* to be developed by the method of characteristics for gas expansion—something we all had to learn in our Gas Dynamics class.

I asked George if that was what it was or if it represented the complex way he, or someone, determined the exact and proper shape of the shuttle's nose. He laughed uproariously and brushed away the cigarette ashes that were victims of his laughter; they fell onto the drawing board. He bent over and handed me a French curve and said half coughing, "No, it's the number of the French curve I used to draw the nose."

It was then that my disillusionment started. All of these math courses, all of the equations and complexity we were forced to master in engineering school, and then I find out it's all done with *French curves*. I started to realize that even though the world can be described mathematically, it is usually drawn "close enough" with French curves.

* * *

Another dose of the real aerospace world came just a few weeks later. One of my colleagues told me that a guy in our Wind Tunnel Operations group, Frank, was going to retire. I knew Frank. He sat a couple rows behind me. He was independently wealthy and made no bones about not needing the job. He even refused to join the Bond Drive, which really ticked off the managers because they wanted 100 percent participation from the group. Frank told them that he didn't become a millionaire by investing in savings bonds. But his experience was invaluable to them; he was needed and was, frankly, tolerated by the management. With all that, he still came across as a very mild-mannered, quiet kind of a guy. Nice guy actually, just didn't like management.

The whole Wind Tunnel Group was going to take Frank out to lunch that Friday. We all went to a small Mexican place with linoleum tables and floor and we sat with Frank and ate "Tack-os" and burritos that we ordered from the counter. I happened to sit next to Frank and talked to him about his retirement. This occasion seemed so, well, like old-timer stuff to me. But I was half curious, as in what it was like to be retiring, and half just being polite. In the course of our conversation, I asked Frank, "So when is your retirement dinner?" Unfortunately, it was one of those instances when all talking just happened to cease as I asked my question. The whole group heard me and they all started to bellow out laughs that quickly made me shrink into my clothes.

He waited for the laughter to die down and then Frank replied with, "You don't understand, Bill; *this* is it!"

"But what about the gold watch and the speech for your thirty-two years?" I said.

He laughed. Someone else in the group said, "Bill, this is aerospace; he's lucky he survived thirty-two years; forget the watch."

Frank nodded in agreement with a look of resignation. A look that said, This is just the way it is kid; nothing personal.

That bothered me for quite some time.

20

Because the shuttle program was a NASA program, NASA insisted that we use their facilities. This meant using wind tunnels at NASA Ames in Mountain View, California (nice duty), Langley in Virginia (OK duty), Lewis in Cleveland (not so great duty during the winter). But sometimes it was impractical to use these facilities due to schedule conflicts or if technical requirements like the model size or wind speed (Mach number) didn't match the capabilities of these tunnels. In those cases the next choice was to use the U.S. Air Force facilities. Most of the Air Force wind tunnels were near Tullahoma, Tennessee, at the Arnold Engineering and Development Center (AEDC).

The Air Force had their little pet projects that they were testing like, probably, the F-117 or the B-2 bomber (unbeknownst to us at the time) and probably others that we still know nothing about.

The NASA, or non-Air Force, projects had a low priority. So the Air Force allowed NASA and its contractors—that would include me—to use their facilities around the Fourth of July, Labor Day, Thanksgiving, and Christmas. That way the Air Force guys got the holidays off. Did I mention that these tests lasted about three weeks, give or take? Sometimes being the "owner" has its privileges.

For each wind tunnel test, the model was inspected at the B-1 Division near LAX where it was fabricated. I had to be sure the profiles were correct, that the control surfaces could be deflected as required, and that the model was complete and ready to ship.

It was boxed in a crate built especially for the model, shipped to the wind tunnel, unpacked, prepped, and installed into the wind tunnel test section. The time involved was directly proportional to the size of the model and how many instruments were on it. Mine usually had hundreds and required about four days to hook up.

The testing was laid out by the test engineer, me, to make the most efficient use of the expensive wind tunnel time. So, for example, all the same Mach number runs were grouped together. The other variables were things like the shuttle configuration, e.g., orbiter, orbiter plus tank, orbiter plus tank plus solid rockets; or the pitch, roll, yaw attitude of the vehicle and elevon, speed brake, body flap, or rudder deflections.

The time spent in Downey was either writing post-test reports documenting the tests or preparing pretest reports that outlined the model, Mach number, instruments, run schedule, and settings that were to be accomplished for the next model or test.

For four and a half years I did this—dozens of three-week trips missing various holidays. I didn't feel too bad though. I knew some guys that spent a year and a half at AEDC doing B-1 bomber variable inlet tests (and then they decided to build the B-1 with a fixed inlet to save money).

We usually stayed at the Holiday Inn in Manchester, Tennessee. Right off the freeway as you entered town was a privately owned liquor store selling gifts, girlie magazines, milk, bibles—something for everyone. In front of the store was a life-size plastic horsey with a motorized front leg that went up and down and up and down for, I think, fifty years. It never stopped. Every trip, up and down and up and down; rain or snow, up and down and up and down; Christmas Day, up and down and up and down.

The Waffle House was popular, mainly because it was open twenty-four hours, which supported our graveyard schedule. And the food, it was quite edible. When I walked into the Waffle House for the first time, circa 1973, I had the then chic long hair, my standard issue black horn-rimmed glasses, and a left eyeball that kept looking for falling objects to the right. I was, at that time, quite an attractive guy; just a downright California babe magnet.

Manchester was a typical southern town, I guess, with the court house in the center and the square of the town's main streets surrounding it. On the courthouse steps were a bunch of old guys whittling sticks. I was about twenty-four at the time, and these guys must have been fifty at least. I was forewarned by the other more experienced engineers not to talk to them; they didn't like Calee-forn-yunz, I was told.

Several trips later we brought along a "newbie" test engineer. His name was Jose; he had a strong Mexican accent, was a good engineer and fun to be around. His first day in Manchester he walked up to the guys whittlin' and talked to them, even though one of our guys warned him. He was interested in the Civil War and one of the whittlers took him inside the city hall and showed him some historical stuff on display. Another man came up and asked him his name, where he was from and all. Jose told him and beamed with excitement over seeing the Civil War memorabilia. The man invited him to his house for dinner to see more Civil War stuff. It was the mayor! So we, the veteran engineers, stayed home and watched Jose get picked up and driven to the mayor's home for a fabulous dinner and the chance to look at lots of memorabilia. Lesson learned: Don't believe what others say about whittlers, or anyone for that matter; make your own assessment.

I tested several different space shuttle models in Tullahoma, all of them in the AEDC Von Karmen Facility (VKF) wind tunnels; usually tunnel A or C. There was a B too. Once there was an armed guard at the entrance to the test section of the B tunnel. He had an M-16 and there was a sign that said he could and would kill you. We waved. He didn't smile and fortunately he didn't shoot. We guessed he was guarding some secret airplane model they were testing.

These wind tunnels were the type that recirculated the air, so the air just went around in a giant circle, albeit at Mach 2 plus. In one of the tunnels a technician left a stepladder in the test section and they failed to see it on the TV monitors before they started the wind tunnel. The ladder got sucked into the big turbine engines that circulate the air. What a mess! It took months to repair the damage.

21

Lockheed **was responsible for** making the thermal protection tiles for the Orbiter. These things were really something. There was a photo in *Aviation Week* magazine, the trade magazine of aerospace, showing someone holding this red- hot tile with his fingers on the corners. The big deal was for it to act as an insulator and to be as light weight as possible.

Our wind tunnel testing also included dynamics testing. There was a concern that these tiles, reported to be quite fragile, would crack or get shaken off the Orbiter from the vibration and from the aerodynamic forces. So they devised a wind tunnel test that would use the actual tiles.

Some guy from Lockheed brought down a sample tile, a real one, for us to examine and to be sure we were making the wind tunnel model to correctly match the dimensions of the tiles.

The guy carried a bright silver, very sturdy-looking metal briefcase. He carefully opened the latches and lifted the lid. Black foam lay beneath. There on the bottom half of the brief case was a very white square. It looked like a flat, white bathroom tile. He donned some white gloves and lifted it from the case by the corners. It was then we could see that it was only a few inches thick. He lifted it like it was nitroglycerin and gently set it on the desk. The Lockheed guy turned to answer a question from someone. While he was turned away, one of the guys couldn't resist and he lightly tapped the center of the tile. It shattered into a thousand pieces! Someone yelled, "Uh-oh!"

"What did you do!?" the Lockheed guy yelled as he spun around.

"Nothing; I just touched it!" he said.

"You broke it. Why did you do that?"

I said, "Hey, I watched him, he touched it like it was tissue paper."

He got the foam-lined suit case and scraped the body fragments and dust back into the case, snapped it closed, and left mumbling something about bumbling North American Rockwell engineers.

Six weeks later an article in *Aviation Week* said that Lockheed missed their tile delivery schedule since they had a "brittleness" issue.

* * *

Wind tunnel model 26 OT was a pressure model of the Orbiter (O) and the large External Tank (T). It was to collect pressure data on the various surfaces of the vehicle and correlate the pressure with the temperature data.

The model was too small to mount the pressure instrumentation inside as usually done so I told the designers to mount them in a box on the back of the sting, the strut that holds the model into the wind stream. The wind tunnel air was preheated to about 1,500 degrees F to simulate flight, so I had to be sure the instruments didn't melt.

I designed a box that would be cooled by spraying water on the outside. The water would travel across the box and cool it. This "film cooling" is used a lot in rocket engine design. (Gee, I wonder how I got that idea …Fridays in the library at Parks College paid off.)

The model was installed in the NASA Ames 3.5 foot Hypersonic Wind Tunnel in Mountain View, California. This wind tunnel was a "blow-down" tunnel meaning high pressure compressed air was stored in tanks. Opening a few valves would allow air to travel to a test section where the model was suspended. It is like a deflating balloon, and there is just so much compressed air. Another feature of wind tunnels is that when they start, the mother of all shock waves comes down the pipe and whacks everything in sight, including delicate models; it would rip most models right off the mounting sting. To get around this characteristic, most super or hypersonic wind tunnels are designed with a device to insert and retract the model only after the tunnel flow is stabilized.

Pressures were recorded by a mechanical device that took up to ninety seconds to sample all of the model pressures. So there was a race between getting all of the data and retracting the model before the air was depleted and the shockwave ripped the model off the sting.

Author with Orbiter pressure model; 1975
Courtesy NASA/Ames

We got the model all hooked up and ready for the first test. I turned on the water remotely and the model was retracted out of the way so we could start the air flow. The valves opened and the roar of the demon shock wave rumbled the floor. After the shock wave was gone and when the pressure stabilized, the operator, Jerry, inserted the model into the air stream. It was visible on closed circuit TV. When it hit the center line the pressure sampling device started and I started a stopwatch.

The nose of the model started to glow white on the black and white screen from the preheated air. The temperature in the box was a nice sixty degrees.

Thirty seconds. The pressures were still being recorded. Forty seconds. We had about another seventy seconds of air. But then, suddenly, I saw one of the wind tunnel pressure gauges start to fluctuate. Jerry saw it too. We heard the roar of the shock monster, but far off. What was going on? We had plenty of time left.

Thirty seconds to go. Another gauge started to fluctuate; then another. The roar became louder.

"PULL IT OUT!" I yelled. Jerry hit the EMERGENCY RETRACT button.

WHAM! A *huge* thud of something hit the rear wall of the tunnel. I winced thinking the model had been ripped off the sting and slammed against the exhaust end of the wind tunnel. But the model was still there.

The airflow stopped, we opened the test cell door, and went into the test section to investigate what caused that horrific sound. Jerry crawled on his belly down the exit "pipe," where the air goes after it passes the model. I could hear his belt and some tools scraping the metal cylinder as he crawled into the abyss, eventually ending up near the entrance to huge spheres that "caught" the air. The light from his flashlight got dimmer and dimmer. I heard him say with a bunch of echoes, "Holy shit!"

As he inched through the narrow, dark pipe I could hear him grunting and something scraping, like he was pushing something along the pipe. I looked at the model. Everything was intact. What could have fallen off that he was dragging back? He emerged with a gigantic piece of *ice*! It had to be fifty or sixty pounds! How could this be? Fifteen hundred degrees Fahrenheit at the nose of the model, but ice?

Then it occurred to me: I was squirting water into a Mach 5 air stream; it froze and a huge ice ball grew on the back of the box, just outside of the TV monitor's view. The ice was blocking the air flow and the monster shock wave was right behind it. When we retracted the model, the ice was sheared off.

I turned down the water flow; next test, just a little bit of ice. Problem solved. We thought of putting beer or something in there to chill it.

A few months later, there was a rather large article in *Aviation Week* (Aviation Leak, as we used to call it) about the shuttle wind tunnel tests. There were lots of photos of models in wind tunnels and there was a picture of mine!

* * *

Joyce and I took our first vacation in 1974. We went from our apartment in Norwalk, California, to Zion and Bryce National Parks, up to Salt Lake City, Jackson Hole, then back across Nevada to Tahoe and Yosemite. Two weeks camping, well, most of the time, with everything stowed in the Duster's huge trunk. Unfortunately Joyce and I took only a few vacations like that over the next thirty-plus years. While we liked them, and who wouldn't, we struggled with financial priorities.

We talked about having kids when we were engaged, but after we were married neither one of us even brought it up for at least a few years. Neither of us had that burning paternal urge. We thought we had plenty of time to decide whether to start our own family.

✱ ✱ ✱

I still liked to build model rockets and spent a good deal of time in the extra bedroom at a desk that my grandfather had commissioned the Aliquippa Senior High wood shop make for him. Sitting there, I sanded a lot of balsa wood fins.

Being in the wind tunnel testing group I discovered that during subsonic testing they would put oil, black oil, on a white model or the other way around too. The wind would move the oil and trace the airstreams; therefore, it was called oil flow visualization.

So why not do that with a model rocket? I built a white rocket, got some linseed oil, added black dye, and put different size dots all over the model. I launched it and was successful at grabbing the model by the parachute so the tall grass wouldn't mess up the oil. And there they were, oil tracks that mapped the aerodynamic flow over and around the rocket! They were terrific! I wrote a paper and sent it in to *Model Rocketry* magazine. They published it and little did I know that someone would remember this paper many years later.

My rocket projects got more and more challenging. I got the idea to make a model rocket of the space shuttle. Hey, why not? I had the drawings. After hundreds of hours planning, calculating, replanning, designing, and redesigning, I finally started to build it.

The complexity was high. I broke my cardinal rule of "keep it simple" frankly because this was not a simple configuration; it was extremely difficult to model. I worked on it off and on for a few years. When I ran tests at the Ames three-and-a-half-foot wind tunnel, during my time off I would sit at a work bench right next to the wind tunnel nozzle working on my models; usually I worked on the shuttle model.

When I supported other test engineers' tests, I helped by manning a shift and following their direction. So I would come in around 11:00 a.m., work on my space shuttle model rocket until around 3:00 p.m., and then do my swing shift until midnight.

On one test we'd been there six very long weeks. We were supposed to do all three Mach numbers, 5, 7 and 10, but the Mach 10 stuff was third priority and we were pooped; plus, the thermal guys said they had enough data. So after another week we packed up and came home.

The next test in line was some NASA test at Mach 10. As we were packing they had already moved the huge Mach 10 nozzle in place and were torquing the bolts with a pneumatic air wrench, just like the auto mechanics at Sears.

A few days later, after the weekend, we got word that there was an explosion at the three-and-a-half-foot wind tunnel at the NASA Ames facility, with one minor injury. All wind tunnel testing had been canceled until further notice.

The explosion had blown off all of the large garage doors, and all of the tables, chairs, tools, drill presses, lathes, cans, rags, etc., were blown out into the parking lot about a hundred feet away. The lathe was torn from the concrete floor and went about eighty feet.

Had we run Mach 10, and had they started Mach 10 on a day when I was sitting where I normally sat working on my models, next to the lathe, I'd be dead.

Of course there was an investigation. It revealed that the bolts that held the nozzle onto the test section had been unknowingly overstressed.

I still thought of the NASA Ames work bench in the parking lot crumpled up like a piece of aluminum foil next to the lathe. Now, no one is allowed near the wind tunnel when it is being operated. Oh yeah, the person with minor injuries was Jerry, the tech; he sat on one of the red hot pebbles that they used to heat the air.

I told my close-call story to my supervisor, and he told his manager; in that way, word got out that I was building a flying model of the space shuttle. About a week later the manager and the aerodynamics supervisor and another PhD aerodynamicist came to my desk and asked about my model. I brought in photos of the current assembly state and told them it wouldn't be long before I was going to do some Orbiter test flights (free flight). They were very interested.

About a month later, Ellis Chee and I went to a field and we test flew the Orbiter model. After several attempts we finally had it trimmed so it would fly; well, as best as a brick with wings could fly. I told the interested parties about the results and they were really happy to hear about the success. They asked several questions and seemed genuinely grateful that I shared the information with them. The space shuttle was the most complex and non-rocket-looking launch vehicle ever devised. The designers wanted to get their hands on any information or test results, from any source. It was hard to imagine that my hobby project of the space shuttle would have some, albeit miniscule, input to the program, but it did.

After that, I put my shuttle model on hold for a bit.

* * *

Joyce and I shared our '72 Plymouth Duster. This was a time when folks usually had one car. Joyce was working on her B.A. degree in social welfare and commuted to California State, Long Beach. She would drop me off early in the morning and then pick me up at 4:42, my quitting time. Joyce was known in our apartment complex as "the girl with the long brown hair and sunglasses."

Between my wind tunnel trips, we occasionally shared some evenings and a few Thanksgivings with some friends from Rockwell. We went back to La Grange, IL, near Chicago, once or twice to see Joyce's parents.

A year or so after we left for L.A., Dad was transferred again, this time from the J&L Hammond plant, where he successfully helped pull the plant back to life, to another J&L rolling mill in Boardman, Ohio, near Youngstown. They bought a nice house and I occasionally visited them when I was flying back from a wind tunnel test at Langley Research Center in Virginia.

I wrote them a few letters describing in great detail what I did and all about the shuttle program. Years later I found them in my scrapbook that Mother had put together. She loved those letters, I could tell.

* * *

After four years at North American Rockwell Joyce and I went to the rollout of the first shuttle orbiter, "Enterprise." We were amused because the "Trekies" wanted the first space shuttle to be named Enterprise. Too bad the first one was for atmospheric test flights only and would never see space. We *tried* to tell them.

The rollout meant a lot to me. I could see things on the orbiter that were directly related to tests that I had run in the years I spent there. Seeing the final product made it all worthwhile and this would be a theme throughout my entire career.

A year or so prior to the rollout, I recall a lot of talk around the coffee machine about the perplexing problem of how to get the orbiter into the air to do subsonic atmospheric and landing tests. These tests were to be the first flight tests years before a shuttle liftoff with rocket engines.

We saw all sorts of concepts. One was to take two C-5 airplanes, cut the left wing off of one and the right wing off of the other, put the two C-5s next to one another, and bridge them together with a straight wing or beam structure. The orbiter would hang under this center beam. Now *that* would have been something.

I heard some guys, as they looked at their coffee cup poker hands, laughing about some aerodynamicist that came up with an idea to put the orbiter on the back of a 747 and have it lift off the top of it. Yeah, right! All everyone visualized was the orbiter sliding backwards clipping off the vertical tail and, well, disaster.

But this aerodynamicist persisted and insisted that this would work. A year or so later, the 747 with the orbiter mounted on its back took off from Edwards Air Force Base. The 747 pilots kept asking if the orbiter was still there because it was so light they could hardly feel it.

There were lots of managers holding their breaths when the orbiter separated from the 747. What a sight! In essence the orbiter dropped the 747 and it worked fine. The aerodynamicist was right. Sometimes it pays to stick to your guns. But he still had to use his supervisor's hall pass to go to the bathroom.

* * *

It was gratifying to see how the wind tunnel tests that we ran with just a handful of people contributed directly to the design of the space shuttle. It made the all-nighters when we wired up instrumentation at the wind tunnel and the many weeks away from home worthwhile. I was not involved in the data reviews or the decision making processes that resulted in these important shuttle design conclusions. Nevertheless, it meant a lot to me to just be a part of it, albeit small.

An Aerospace Leaf Blower and
Flames the Size of North Dakota

22

My career plan at North American Rockwell was simple: do wind tunnel testing, do orbiter flight testing at Edwards, and then launch operations at Cape Kennedy—to be one of the console guys. But when it came time for people to transfer to Edwards for the orbiter drop tests my director wouldn't let me go. He said I was one of two or three guys left doing aerodynamic heating testing and I was too valuable to let go. Several others were laid off over the four years I was there; others transferred out.

I called a friend who had quit Rockwell a few months earlier. He put in a good word for me at his new company, Acurex, and I received a phone call and a letter of invitation for an interview.

I took a vacation day, put on my suit, and flew to San Jose, California, on PSA airlines. I drove up Route 101 and went to the Mountain View plant; it was right next to the Sunnyvale golf course on the final approach to the Moffett Field Navy base, and home of NASA Ames where I had run many of my space shuttle wind tunnel tests.

The receptionist called my point of contact and I was led to a conference room with no less than a dozen people around a large conference table. I sat at the only remaining seat, the one with the water glass plus pitcher at the head of the table. Each had a copy of my resume. They were poor copies; crooked, with a low-cartridge faded streak running the length of the paper and a bent over corner complete with a Xeroxed paperclip. So much for using good paper.

One guy suggested we go around the room and introduce ourselves. I was last. Each said his name, rank, serial number, so to speak, and when they got to me, to try to break this huge ice cube in the room, I asked with a big smile if there was a quiz at the end? Nothing. Hmm, not going well so far.

Halfway through my rather short "who I am, what I did, and why I want to come here speech" a guy slaps his dime store portfolio closed and leaves.

I stopped.

Another said, "Your resume states you graduated from Parks College and yet your application shows you also attended the University of Pittsburgh; what other things did you misrepresent on your resume?"

Ahhhh, I get it, I thought. They're trying to piss me off. They want to see how I'll hold up under pressure.

"No misrepresentation," I said. "A resume is an overview not a complete history. I didn't list my elementary school either, which you asked on your application. On the interview more background details can be discussed. And, frankly, there wasn't room on the paper."

"You stated that you designed a rocket engine at Parks College. What method did you use to calculate the nozzle throat boundary layer conditions? Did you consider viscous effects and the impact of that on the effective nozzle throat size and thrust coefficient?"

"No, it was a demonstration engine not flight hardware." He got up and walked out stating, "You won't fit in my group."

After the door closed, someone else asked, "How did you arrive at the nozzle throat diameter?"

"The throat diameter was selected by the available drill bit size in the machine shop. I backed out performance parameters from that."

This went on for two hours. One by one they left in a huff. I was proud of myself that I stayed centered and didn't lose my temper. Finally two guys were left: the test guy and his boss, the group I wanted to work for in the first place. I really didn't care about those other analysis groups and I said on my application that I wanted to do testing. Well, I held my own anyway.

Just as I was starting discussions about my testing experience in more detail, one of them came back into the room. It was the first guy who stormed out earlier after he said that I wouldn't fit in with his group. He was a very intense man and asked me, "How did you arrive at the nozzle throat diameter on the rocket engine you designed?"

I was at the end of my rope. I looked at him and said, "Well, just after you stormed off in a big huff to try to make me feel bad, I said I used the available drill bit sizes for the throat, and no I did not consider nor did I give a rat's ass about boundary layer effects for a heavy weight engine that put out a measly ten pounds of thrust. And, spare me any more questions because frankly *I* don't want to work in *your* group."

He got up and left. The two test guys were smiling. One said, "He deserved that."

Sooooo, why do I want to work here? was the thought going through my head. The impact of the experience was setting in; I was trying to hold up, but I wanted to flee. This was the feeling I should have noticed and listened to more closely.

The test guys talked to me and that seemed to go OK, although they made no apologies for the way I was treated earlier. Walking out they said they would "probably" make me an offer.

I did get the offer and it was a 20 percent raise. I was to be in a nice office with only one roommate, a window over the golf course, beer night every Friday; a small company with room for advancement. What's wrong with this picture?

But my gut told me no. It yelled, it screamed: NO! But I went by the data, or rather the offer that was on paper; I didn't trust my gut.

They moved us from our apartment in Norwalk, California to an apartment in Mountain View, California, the Greendale Apartments, in only a few weeks. Joyce had graduated from Cal State Long Beach with a BA in social welfare a few months earlier; so this was good timing for her too.

My first assignment was to be the test engineer responsible for a test of a quarter scale model of a cooling torus (donut) that went around the older style nuclear reactors.

They were afraid that if there was an extreme surge in the reactor core (like a meltdown?) the water in the cooling tubes would instantly turn to steam; this would blast down some feeder tubes and enter this huge metal donut half filled with nuked water lifting the whole donut off of its mounting brackets, and then come crashing down; this would break the donut and spew nuked water all over the place. Not good. Of course I always wondered why they just didn't bolt it down; nah, too simple.

The current test engineer was moving to another program so I was the rookie called up to run the rest of "his" tests. Now I could see why he ran the first few tests (one a day) with me watching. I followed him around like a puppy dog watching, learning, and asking why don't you let me do this or that? Nope. Finally after twenty-seven tests—that's *twenty-seven* tests, ladies and gentlemen—he finally "let me" run one; a real vote of confidence. This test setup had one load cell (glorified bathroom scale), a couple of pressure transducers (my wind tunnel tests had lots more), and a few other instruments that were not a big deal. Frankly, I was baffled that he wouldn't let go of this; but then again, it was his baby.

There was some PhD guy on the nuke project; late thirties, curly hair, always running around with papers in his hand to impress everyone how busy he was and, hence, how important he was.

After about my fifth solo test I discovered a problem with the load cell. I analyzed the data, graphed it, and made some charts. As I was practicing my presentation about the problem and my proposed solution, the curly haired PhD guy came into my office. He said there was a meeting upstairs about the "anomaly" and did I have any data. I showed him my data and told him I had a presentation and was ready to brief whoever was interested. He grabbed the charts I made and went into the conference room, with me following again like a puppy dog.

He went directly to the front of the room and started giving my presentation to the managers! With *my* charts! He never said anything about me. Not a peep. I was younger with much more ego then.

Then he said, "We (wow, a concession!) found that the load-bearing surface of the instrument had a high static coefficient of friction normal to the centerline that produced an irregularity in the load cell bridge resistance, and, hence, the measurements were incorrect."

What an ass. I blurted out, "In other words, it was stuck." Everyone laughed. He got all red. New rule: better to simplify, be clear, and not look like a pompous ass. The idea should be to communicate to everyone, not to try to look smart. Einstein once said, "If a seven year old can't understand your theory, it's no good."

And another new rule: if I make the charts, I make the presentation (unless I don't want to). This guy sounded so ridiculous trying to use techno-mumbo-jumbo to describe a stuck load cell and, yes, everything he said was true, but he made it sound so hard. What a phony.

In addition to this nuke testing I was asked to design, build and checkout a "Poor Man's Wind Tunnel." This was 1977 and there was another "The Russians are coming, the Russians are coming" laser scare. The Air Force, frightened about our airplanes and stuff getting zapped by Russian lasers, wanted to fire a laser at different targets like skins of our aircraft, canopies, missiles, and fuel tanks to see how vulnerable they might be. But the problem was, this testing was to be with the airplane parts firmly attached to the ground.

They asked Acurex to build a glorified leaf blower, or rather a Poor Man's Wind Tunnel, to blow air over the parts, and Acurex asked me to build it. Why? I was a wind tunnel test engineer from North American Rockwell and that was good enough for them.

I studied the requirements and laid out some concepts. My budget was $100K and I had to deliver it in six to eight months.

This "leaf blower" had to vary the air speed from Mach 0.1 to 1.0. This meant I had to use a control valve. Knowing absolutely nothing about valves, I had to dive into the vendor library and find companies that made them, order their catalogs, and talk to their sales guys. There was no internet. There were no computers on our desks. Slide rules, maybe a calculator and lots of catalogs; those were the tools of the day. I had tremendous anxiety about this. It was me, myself, and I to figure this out and to make it work. I worked this job at the same time as the nuke job. I would come to work in the morning, the nuke test engineer would set everything up, and run the test with me watching; then at 9:30 a.m. I went up to my office to work on the glorified leaf blower.

After a few months the Poor Man's Wind Tunnel director called me into his office and told me that they were pleased with my progress on the project and couldn't wait for me to go to New Mexico for the four months of installation and testing. "Really? Four months?"

I was finding that this company was just not a fit for me. All the PhDs and "everything is hard" attitude (gets more money from customers) just didn't sit well with me. I knew I didn't like the place during the interview but I went for the money. New rule: Trust your gut with job changes…or anything for that matter.

At the onset, I had made it quite clear that I was not going to do extended travel. So this four-month gig was the last straw for me. Acurex was a good company; it just wasn't a fit for me.

I started looking for another job and four months after I started, I left Acurex and went to work at United Technologies Corporation, Chemical Systems Division, UTC/CSD.

On my last day at Acurex I shipped the Poor Man's Wind Tunnel; I had spent $40K. So I did it for half the budget and in half the time. I saw a guy I knew at Acurex at a supermarket one day a few years later. He told me that the Air Force liked my project so much they ordered four more. He also said that they had given me half of the time and budget to work with, so I made lots of money for them. Next new rule: Don't underestimate yourself.

23

The United Technologies plant was east of San Jose near the town of Coyote. It meant a fifty-minute commute but this was a rocket test and manufacturing plant. This just had to be heaven; rocket design and test. The interview went quite well and I was excited to start work there. I noticed a distinct difference in the feeling in my gut—in a good way.

On my first day I walked into my new office, which was in a trailer, and on my desk was a blotter, pencils, paper, pens, paper clips, erasers, graph paper, and rulers all neatly piled. Someone took the time to pull this together. With that and other things, I have never felt so welcomed on a first day on a job, even to this day.

I was hired as a test engineer responsible for conducting ramjet static tests. A ramjet is a very simple rocket propulsion system. Air from the atmosphere is literally rammed into a cylinder at one end, fuel is injected and ignited and exhausted out the other end. It has to be going very fast, at least above the speed of sound, for this to work.

These tests were done in a large static test facility that provided lots of compressed air and propane to heat the air to simulate the missile traveling through the atmosphere.

My job as the test conductor was to integrate the ramjet with the facility and conduct the test without screwing anything up. Being the new guy, I just observed the first few ramjet tests. I noticed that the preparations were pretty chaotic. There was no formality at all. So I gathered all of the clip boards with the "things to do before ignition" lists and I wrote out a countdown. This went over big. I felt like I was back in the Aliquippa Rocket Club.

There was a team of about a dozen people dedicated to these tests including technicians, computer data acquisition people, and mechanical engineers. One feature about the way this was set up was that the test engineer was the boss. When it came to the test, he or she could order even a manager to do something (not usually done in practice, but it was made clear that that authority was there).

My supervisor was "Zoomie." He got that nickname because when he worked at the Lockheed Santa Cruz facility in the '60s he was a rocket technician. He was on a tall rocket test stand fueling a rather large liquid rocket in preparation for a static test. There was a fuel leak and the Klaxon went off signaling everyone to get the hell off the test stand. There were five guys below him on lower levels. He was the first one on the ground; hence, Zoomie.

He was tall and thin and was used several times to check out the large Titan III solid rocket motors before every static test. These huge motors had a hole in the propellant that went the entire length of the nearly one-hundred-foot-long booster rocket. Before the test they wanted to be sure that the propellant had no cracks or voids so they needed someone to inspect it. Enter Zoomie. They lowered him down the center of the solid propellant inside the vertically standing rocket. They gave him a flashlight and a headset. Even the thought of doing that creeped me out.

* * *

I was assigned as the test conductor for the Advanced Strategic Air Launched Missile (ASALM) ramjet engine test after only witnessing two. They showed a lot more confidence in me than the previous company. There were a couple of Air Force officers, customers, in the observation room waiting patiently with our senior management. They arrived at 1:00 p.m. because they were told, by me, that it would be a 2:00 p.m. test firing. Two o'clock came and went; three o'clock; four o'clock. Finally, I felt it was time to explain in person why we were delayed. I took off my headset and went into the observation room and was quickly reminded by one of the Air Force customers that I told them the firing would be at two.

"Ohhhhh, I'm sorry," I said, "that was 'test time'; 'real time' would be 5:00 p.m."

Even the president of our division couldn't hold back a smile. The

Air Force officer laughed out loud and said that he forgot about the time difference. He knew testing.

The thirty-minute countdown started and we performed numerous operations like cycling valves, bleeding propellant lines, and circulating liquid oxygen. We finally got down to the last few minutes in the countdown.

"Attention, a ramjet test will be conducted on the Coco test stand (that's what we called it); all personnel clear the test stand area," I announced over the area P.A. Fire trucks were stationed, security blocked off the access to the stand, and everyone was ready.

"Mark, T-60 seconds, auto sequence start," I said as I hit the switch on the console. The auto sequence start switch automatically started the steam, air flow, and ramjet ignition in the proper sequence. The huge steam valves started to open and white steam flowed vertically from the ejector. The room started to shake.

"Good steam pressure; exhaust manifold pressure decreasing," one of the techs said. Everything was going as planned.

"T minus forty seconds," I announced.

"T minus thirty seconds." The propane and liquid oxygen valves were opened and the heater was ignited. A muffled boom competed with the other deafening roars now filling the control room as the propane ignited.

"T minus twenty seconds."

The air temperature was stabilizing. We did a final check on the flow rates. Everything looked good. The facility was now simulating high speed flight and high altitude for the ramjet to be ignited.

"Five...four...three...two...one...ignition," I announced. Wham! A flame the size of North Dakota came out of the exhaust with a roar that brought every living critter near the test stand to its feet; the ramjet started.

"Mark, T plus five seconds." A billowing cloud of steam poured from the steam ejector and the rocket exhaust. The noise and vibration even inside the control room was incredible. Then, at T plus fourteen seconds a tremendous roar came over my headset. I looked at the TV monitor and there was fire all over the test stand! The ramjet casing burned through and the 5,000 degree F gases escaped. It burned everything like it was butter. I hit the "fuel off" switch, the air diversion switches to stop the air flow, and started the "deluge" that hosed down the test stand with water. Slowly the roaring beast calmed down and stopped.

But in the control room Art, the supervisor of the electrical technicians, was coming at me with a strange look on his face. And he had scissors in his hand! Before I could even react, he swooped in and sliced off my necktie. It was hung with the others complete with the program, test number, date, and, of course, my name. This is a rocket test tradition; I had soloed and was now an official CSD test conductor. After the test stand was secured, it was traditional for the test crew to go to a pizza place and celebrate a completed test, despite the outcome.

* * *

I was the test conductor for several of these tests and was getting worried that I would never get to see a test firing with my own eyes. So I volunteered for the "roof observer's" job. The roof observer was, well, just that. He was responsible for informing the test conductor if there was a burn-through, explosion, fire, etc. Sometimes the test conductor is looking at data, a gauge, or another person in the control room and might not see that on the monitor the test stand is on fire! Enter the roof observer.

We found, however, that after the steam started at T-60 seconds, there was no way that the test engineer or the roof observer could communicate because there was too much noise outside. So we agreed that the roof observer would just key his microphone on and the blast of noise in the test conductor's ears was a hint that something was amiss; that was the loud noise I had heard during the previous tests that alerted me to the situation on the test stand. The system worked.

I asked the guy that was our expert roof observer if I could do it and he said, "Sure!" I was a little concerned because he agreed so quickly. The rest of the time he was the supervisor of the electrical technicians; I mean, it's not like they hired people to do just that one thing, aerospace or not.

He looked at me and asked, "Are you *sure* you want to do this?" Being the twenty-eight-year-old that I was, I agreed to be the official roof observer for the next test. He took me to the top of the control room roof. It was a flat tar and gravel roof with about a four-inch berm around the edge. I donned the headset, checked in with the test conductor and stretched out on the roof next to the edge about two hundred feet line-of-sight distance to the ramjet. With a pair of binoculars I could see everything on the test stand quite clearly.

"T minus two minutes," I heard over the headset.

"Final status check," the test conductor called reading my countdown procedure.

"Data Recording?"

"Ready."

"Lox Panel?"

"Ready."

"Roof observer?"

"Gotcha covered." (Traditional answer)

"Standby for Auto Sequencer start."

"Three…two…one…mark. Auto sequence start, T minus sixty seconds."

The steam valve opened and that was the last thing I heard over the headset. The steam ejector was very loud and I could feel the heat where I was on the roof. Next, the air started. It was a squealing sound with booms and bangs of valves opening and closing. This was starting to get uncomfortable.

Through the binoculars I saw the Mach diamonds caused by supersonic air screaming out of the diversion valve. I saw the valve rotate diverting the air into the ramjet. A flashbulb mounted on the test stand flashed. That signaled ramjet ignition. An absolutely mammoth roar hit me. My glasses vibrated all over my face. My teeth chattered. My ears, although plugged, ached. I felt every square inch of my body being violated by this beast. The sound intensified. The facility was simulating the acceleration to higher Mach numbers. It screamed. I could feel the utter speed of this thing even though it was sitting on the test stand. I wanted to cut the buttons off my shirt so I could lie closer to the roof! I managed to keep an eye on the test stand. All I could think of was to avoid wetting my pants! It went on and on and on. Naturally, this would be one of the successful tests. Nearly four hundred seconds. Finally another flash bulb signifying fuel cutoff and the engine stopped. The steam slowed but the air stopped abruptly. Moments later, only the hiss of various nitrogen purges prevailed. It was successful. And it was over.

I was still embossed against the edge of the berm. Dick came running up the ladder only a second after shutdown obviously to see my remains before I could pull myself together. He took one look at me and said, laughing, "Wasn't that fun?"

I never did that again.

* * *

I ended up caving into my ambitions to climb the corporate ladder; I became a project engineer. I transferred to the Ramjet Project Engineering staff of UTC that was located at the Sunnyvale plant. This meant a much shorter commute. Before I transferred I failed to ask what project I would be assigned to.

I had a great going-away party and Jerry Blumenkrancz, the head guy of the test site, told me, "You're going to leave the company within two years. I've seen it happen before; you want to be a project engineer and then the fun is gone and you leave."

On my first day at the Sunnyvale UTC/CSD plant I met Sam (a pseudonym), my new manager. I asked what my project would be. "Here, Bill, why don't you read this." It was a five-page technical report that took ten minutes to read. Later, there were no handouts to read. I went to his office a few times and told him that I really wanted to contribute and should I be seeking work myself. He usually said, "No, I'll come up with something for you." I spent many hours in the test cells helping out the test engineers or other project engineers. This went on for months.

Finally Sam came into my office one Friday afternoon and said, "I'm assigning you to be the project engineer on a ducted rocket-ramjet program and I want you to write the test plan for it." He scoped out the project and turned me loose.

Terrific! I was walking three feet above the ground with excitement. I worked all weekend preparing the plan—at home. What Mach numbers, what propellants, what fuel to air mixture ratios, instrumentation, ground support equipment. It was all there, even a cover letter. I typed it up (still no computers) and bound it in a nice folder.

Monday morning I took it to work and walked into Sam's office as I knocked on the door frame. "Sam, I'd like to go over my plans for the ducted rocket project with you. Can we sit down sometime today?"

Before I could add "and show you what I have prepared," he said, "Nah, I already did it and sent it to the customer this morning. I'll let you do something else later this week." As I walked out of his office I dumped my folder into his trash can. He didn't even notice.

Devastation doesn't even come close. And this happened over and over with this guy. It was like Charlie Brown and the football. I always went and tried to kick it. Why? Because I loved to kick the football. I wanted to kick the football. I wanted to contribute. I wanted to do something, not just sit around making work or reading technical articles.

A few months later I couldn't take it anymore and I quit. I had no job to go to; I just quit. I gave two weeks' notice and after a week another manager, Terry, called me into his office. "Would you be interested in working on solid propellant rocket programs?"

I was elated, but cautious. "What would be my project?" I asked. I learn sometimes.

"I have four solid rocket projects: two small ones, a medium one, and a large one called, appropriately, HIPPO."

"And what would be my part in all of these projects?"

"They would be your total responsibility. I would only intercede if I saw you were doing something stupid or you were blowing your budget, but I want you to control your own budget too."

"Sounds good to me. When do I start?"

"Monday, but on one condition," he said.

"What's that?"

"You agree to work at least a year."

"Deal." And with that I was now a solid rocket project engineer; a *real* rocket scientist.

An hour later I said good-bye to Sam and his ramjets. I found out later that Sam was telling everyone that I betrayed him and I stabbed him in the back by leaving. But he never came to ask me why I left. I approached him and told him face to face that I was leaving because I wanted something tangible to do, something I could sink my teeth into. I learned what not to do as a manager from Sam. He simply could not delegate and he wanted all the fun stuff; rather, he wanted to do everything himself.

In that year I worked on several rocket projects. One was a smokeless, high thrust rocket that was to be used as an anti-tank missile. Another was a gas generator for a Lockheed missile that burned for about a minute. The HIPPO was a rather large, heavy weight rocket that was used to test various propellant combinations. The last one was the test of the tomahawk gimbaled nozzle for the solid rocket boost portion of the flight; that was cool, watching the nozzle pitch up and down, then right and left during a five-second solid rocket burn.

I had a really good time. Terry was a great example of letting me do the job. Sam was still saying I stabbed him in the back nine months later. Terry told me that he was very happy with me; so the other side of the story started to circulate due to my performance working for Terry. But this was a hollow vindication for me.

My year was up and Jerry Blumenkrancz's prediction was correct; it was nearly two years since I left the Coyote plant. UTC was a great company and I really loved what I was doing there and I really liked the company. I just hadn't hit it off with one guy, and he was on the promotion board. I had to move on, but I remember fondly the many people I worked with at that company and the things I did there. I thanked Terry, too, for being such a great boss.

A Satellite that Changed the World

24

I was still at CSD actively looking for another job when the space shuttle was first launched in 1981. The day of the launch turned out to be even more satisfying for me than I would have ever dreamed. For this first flight they mounted cameras on the bottom of the orbiter so they could get a good look at the condition of the large external tank during the ascent and tank separation. Today the tanks are painted a brown or rust color, but on the first launch they painted it white.

I listened to them counting down and an anxiety that I hadn't felt since witnessing the Shepard and Glenn flights came over me. I sighed a little when I thought of how I wanted to be on that launch team at the Cape. But it was just not to be. The liftoff was spectacular and I was astonished by the rapid ascent. What balls those astronauts had flying that vehicle. This was the first time a launch vehicle was to be manned on its first flight. This would have been unheard of twenty years earlier. But that was just not practical with this vehicle; it was very complicated and, frankly, required human control. And I'm sure the pilots just loved that; no more "spam in the can" as the Mercury flights were portrayed in the movie *The Right Stuff,* which came out a few years later.

They showed the ascent via ground camera; then when it got too far away they showed us the live views from the other cameras on the vehicle as it was climbing to orbit. The solid rocket boosters fell away and then the orbiter and the external tank (ET) continued. Several minutes later they called for ET separation and they switched to the camera on the belly of the orbiter looking at the tank. Suddenly there was motion and the tank fell very slowly away from the camera. After it drifted far enough away, you could see the entire length of the tank.

And there, burned into the tank's white paint, was the exact pattern that we saw when we ran phase-change paint wind tunnel tests several years earlier. It looked like a large black burn mark right by the forward strut, then some white as you went aft, and then another spot a little smaller, and so forth all the way down the tank's top centerline.

This was caused by the shock wave bouncing between the orbiter and the external tank during the first few minutes of the launch. Well, it just made my day. It reminded me of my wind tunnel days at North American Rockwell. I felt a great satisfaction having had something to do with this event.

* * *

During that year, I went to an ophthalmologist for an eye exam, the first exam I had had since Pittsburgh. He looked at my eyes and said, "I can fix this." I agreed to surgery and he straightened out my eyes. Well, sort of. The next year I went to another surgeon who was a muscle surgery specialist and he did a pretty good job to correct the alignment of both eyes so I looked at least somewhat normal.

My eyes have since drifted back a little but they are considerably better than when I was in high school. Where were these surgeons then? The ironic thing is that about five or ten years later I could care less about my eyes. If someone didn't know which eye I was looking at them with, then that was their problem. Oh yes, and everything was paid for by the insurance company; no deductible, nothing. The good ol' days.

That same year, 1981, I saw a huge ad in the classified section of the *San Jose Mercury News* that said, in banner letters, "Lockheed Sunnyvale Wants Propulsion Engineers" or something to that effect. The ad said, "Seeking engineers with experience in solid rocket propulsion (got that), liquid rocket propulsion (got that) and testing" (got that too). Hmm; seemed like a fit to me. I wrote a cover letter referencing the ad, attached my resume, and sent it in.

I was interested in the Space Division; I didn't particularly want to work on nukes in the Missile Division. I dressed up with my suit and tie and met Mr. Al Streit, who was the head of the satellite propulsion group. We went to his office; it was a cubicle. He had a standard issue gray desk with a plastic gray laminate covering the top. Years of wear, cigarette trails etched in time, and many scratches from moves over the years adorned the not so elegant piece of furniture. The table matched the desk in every way. Metal book cases lined his cubicle. All except one had crushed down top shelves, as if someone had sat on them.

I sat down and Al started talking. He told me about his experiences at Redstone Arsenal in Huntsville, Alabama, in the fifties and sixties. His accent and the mention of anywhere near Tennessee brought back wind tunnel testing at AEDC and the image of the horsy in Manchester. I just knew that even as Al was talking that horse's leg in Manchester, Tennessee, was still going up and down, up and down.

After forty minutes of Al's stories, he asked if I had any questions. I rattled off some of the typical stuff and the "What will be my first assignment?" led to, "Well, we'll keep you busy for awhile until your clearances come through."

"Then what do I do?"

"Well, I really can't say; it's classified, but I think you'll like it." I asked several more questions, and then I asked him if he had any questions for me.

"No. Just your availabil–ah–T," I told him, and then he shook my hand and that was it.

No questions like: "Where do you want to be five years from now?" or my favorite: "What are your strengths and weaknesses?" He hired me and he gave me some terrific assignments. A few years later I asked him about that day and he said he decided he was going to hire me when I shook his hand when we met in the lobby.

I was in the "ice box" until my clearance came in. This meant I was doing unclassified stuff until I was cleared. Julie Price, my cubicle mate, was assigned "Metrification." The then current administration thought America should go metric. She spent seven months on a metric data base for the propulsion group, which no one used. We didn't go metric.

Julie had a knack for knowing if my all black socks were on inside out or not. This was definitely a gift. Twenty-five years later Julie, a manager, would lift my pant leg and say, "Yup, inside out!" and we'd laugh like we had years before when things were simpler.

Al gave me an assignment to figure out where I would put thrusters on the submarine laser communication satellite (SLCSAT) proposal and calculate the "moments" in each axis, etc. ("Misser Dye, what is moment prease?") I worked on it Monday, did calculations Tuesday and Wednesday, wrote a report on Thursday, polished it Friday, and put it on his desk the following Monday. He told me I did a good job (thank you, Dr. Lin) but he looked kind of thrown. He said he'd have to get back to me later with another assignment. Uh-ho, I think I was supposed to "milk" that last one for a couple of weeks or so, while I waited for my clearance. A few days later Al told me that he liked the report, it was correct, and to go to the SLCSAT Program and be the "propulsion engineer."

This program was in a different building. Lockheed, Sunnyvale, was so busy in the early 1980s with about twenty-five thousand employees that it had to lease office buildings around Mountain View and Sunnyvale. I found the Silicon Valley building: single story with large glass windows, trees surrounding the parking lot, and a casual appearance and feel to the area. These kinds of buildings were everywhere, but later with the ups and downs of Silicon Valley, many would go from full occupancy to sporting "For Lease" signs.

SLCSAT was a proposal for the navy. It was to be a submarine communication satellite with a laser. The laser details were classified but the bus, the part of the satellite that supplied power, attitude control, propulsion, thermal control, and communications, were all unclassified. I had to provide propulsion system inputs to the proposal. This meant I had to select the propulsion hardware as well as prepare the design specifications.

It took a few months and Al held my hand to only a small extent. This was invaluable to me. By not mothering over my every move or decision he showed me that he had confidence in me and that I could do this with minimal supervision; little did I know that this would set me off rapidly on my career path. In other words, I quickly established a reputation for requiring little supervision, which was every supervisor's dream I would find out later. At the time though, I really thought that I was just doing my job.

Alas, the program was canceled. But it was on that program I started to learn about satellites, people, management, and customers. And a twenty-five-year spacecraft journey began.

25

I was finally assigned to an existing program as part of the Propulsion Subsystem group. My supervisor, whom I had met earlier when I was still working for Al, sat down with me and told me that I was to be responsible for the satellite propulsion system components. These included the plumbing, valves, filters and pressure tanks and are necessary to get the propellant from the tanks to the thrusters. This seemed fine to me. He introduced me to Wayne, who was a senior responsible equipment engineer (REE); he would be guiding me and reviewing my work until I got up to speed.

I wrote several specifications for all of these components; the specs detailed how these parts were to function, how they were to be tested, and a myriad of requirements they had to meet. I also had to prepare test procedures that, for example, verified that all the propulsion system components were working on the spacecraft as they should, and that the assembled system had no leaks. This included getting intimately involved in the procedures for loading propellants at the launch base. And this is where a long relationship with the guys at the base began and continued for over twenty years and several programs.

Wayne and others in the propulsion group were very kind and took time to show me the ropes. They told me the rationale for why they did things, so I benefitted from their years of experience. They taught me all the things to look out for in a satellite propulsion system, including proper test philosophies, methods, practices, and documentation. But, most importantly, the "why" for each.

I was introduced to senior engineers in other departments and I quickly became familiar with the processes within the program on how to get things done and how to make and get approval for changes. They emphasized to not take anything for granted and particularly to review test results from vendors, not listen to: "Trust me; it will work fine."

I learned about quality control (some good things, some not so good) and the different specialties like metallurgy, stress/dynamics, contamination, safety, thermal, manufacturing, and procurement. These key specialties, and others, were applied not only to a single propulsion component, but they also applied to the entire propulsion subsystem, other subsystems, and the entire satellite. So mastering the fundamentals of these specialties was key to managing an entire satellite years later. Hardware and test experience is imperative.

It was important that I got to know these specialists. In the future these relationships would be invaluable as I could ask their advice on these specialty topics. I was like a sponge soaking up every bit of information I was taught about satellite liquid propulsion systems: all of the different components, the vendors that made them, their cost, and delivery schedules. Not only did I have to figure out how the system would work once in space, but also how it should be tested on the ground to be sure it would work properly after it was launched.

After a few launches, I worked on a different program that required titanium tubing, instead of stainless, in the propulsion system. This was something new. It was my task to direct the development of a welding process to weld titanium tubing. I worked with the manufacturing guys and after several months we had a system down that was a vast improvement over the old method of joining tubes. The welding process and equipment was adopted and has been used ever since on many spacecraft.

I was also the propellant valve REE. This included the propellant isolation valves (PIVs). These valves isolated various propellant tanks in the spacecraft.

The PIV vendor had a serial number on each valve. Our Lockheed system had its own serial numbers and of course they were mismatched by two. With several valves on order, this was getting confusing. So the vendor's number was, say 001, and the Lockheed serial number for that valve was 003; or, wait, was his 003 and mine 001? We couldn't keep it straight. There were eight valves and we wrestled with this for about two months; finally I asked the Lockheed buyer to write the valve company,

Consolidated Controls, a letter that said: "Until further notice the following valves will be referred to by the names as indicated below":

Vendor Serial Number	Lockheed Serial Number	New PIV Name
001	003	Sleepy
002	004	Sneezy
003	005	Doc
004	006	Dopey
005	007	Happy
006	008	Bashful
007	009	Grumpy
008	010	Snow White

A couple of weeks later I received a call from one of the procurement guys, who hadn't seen the memo. "Hi, Bill, could you explain something kinda strange?"

"Maybe, depends on just how strange it is."

"Well, I just got a call from Consolidated Controls. Jeff wasn't here so I took the call, and, get this, they asked me to tell you that, Grumpy and Sleepy just passed acceptance testing; waiting for leak test results for Doc. And then they asked, What do you want us to do with Snow White?"

"Well, that's good news but tell them to sit on Snow White and ship Doc as soon as his leak tests are done."

"OoooooooK...this is a joke, right?"

After a good laugh I told him about the serial numbers and gave him a copy of the memo. I knew I was destined for more fun with this job especially when he said, "I wish everyone did this; what a way to turn a boring purchasing job into something fun. Thanks!" I felt good *that* day driving home from work.

26

All flight hardware for satellites has to be tested; a lot. An airplane can come back, get repaired and fly again; a spacecraft: wave good-bye and hope it lasts for seven years or for however long the mission is.

The majority of these tests simulate the launch. It's like a blender. There's lots of vibration from the booster rockets, shock—like a sledge hammer strike—from the detonating cord that separates the booster rocket stages; quick venting—the air gets sucked out extremely fast since this thing is "rocketing" up through the atmosphere. You have to be sure that the satellite survives these horrific environments and that the life isn't literally shaken out of the parts.

My propellant isolation valves had to be tested to be sure they would stay closed during the booster ascent. There was a small company that had a bunch of shaker tables located just off the end of one of the Los Angeles airport runways. I flew down to LAX with my valve and drove to this company to do a random vibration test.

I found the facility engineer assigned to my project and we put a flight valve that was allocated for this test on one of the test tables. While waiting in the control room, I noticed a small poster mounted on one of the control room walls. It was a photo of a chimpanzee dressed with a shirt, eyeglasses, and a pocket protector with pens looking like a dopey engineer. He was pointing with his finger planted firmly on a large open book that was lying on a table. The caption read, "It says so right here in the spec."

I absolutely loved this poster. To me it said it all. Any monkey, sorry, chimp, can blindly follow the spec (specification) right off the cliff.

One of the test lab employees said to me, "You're going to have to wait a bit longer in the control room; we're going to test this guy's flight box first."

"OK, I'll just wait my turn."

I glanced at the chimp poster again and waited.

The test engineer said he was ready. I could hear the sound coming from the shaker. The tone got higher and higher in pitch. And then higher…and higher…and higher; then BLAM! The box exploded and then I heard: ting, ting, ting …wall-a-wall-a…boomp as the parts landed on the floor. Inwardly everyone was howling with laughter—I certainly was—but outwardly we all had that concerned professional frown.

The box engineer left the control room and went out to the table. A technician went too. The visiting box engineer stood there in shock as the tech picked up all the pieces and put them into a bucket. He quietly handed the bucket of remains to the engineer then turned to me and said, "NEXT!"

That's when I lost it; I couldn't contain my laughter. It must have been contagious because the bucket toting box engineer started to laugh too; then all the folks in the control room followed.

My test went just fine. As I left I looked one more time at the chimp poster; this I would remember.

* * *

I stayed in Propulsion for three years spending many hours in the "high bay," where satellites are assembled, doing tests on various satellite propulsion systems. As a test engineer or responsible equipment engineer you didn't handle the flight hardware that much. The union technicians did that, but you were responsible for it.

Although I was gaining more experience, I never assumed that I had anywhere near the experience level of the senior guys. Lockheed training was one of the biggest assets in my career. It was invaluable to have several senior people spend so much time with the new folks like me, to train us and bring us up to speed. You just don't see much of that anymore. Too bad; much of the knowledge of the seniors isn't being passed on to the younger engineers. Years later I tried everything I could to encourage this but ended up just doing my own private mentoring sessions with "the kids."

27

My model rockets were getting bigger and I was still trying to find a computer to run a program that would determine if the rocket would fly into the wind as it should.

Lockheed had some Hewlett-Packard machines that used magnetic strips that you used to store your programs on, kind of like nine-inch-long wimpy credit cards with two magnetic strips on a side. In my free time I learned to program the HP machine.

These programs helped me design a large multistage cluster model rocket. Seven motors in the first stage, three motors in the second stage. I called it BB-Shot.

Model rockets can be staged but the motors have to be Scotch-taped together, so the boosters can only be about two inches long. I liked to build models of real rockets or real-looking rockets and this two-inch booster limitation just wouldn't do. BB-shot was going to have a long booster and I needed a way to ignite the upper stage engines as well as recover the booster by parachute. I came up with using a flashbulb, a mercury switch, and a small battery. At booster burnout the mercury switch would fire the flashbulb, which would light three fuses and, whoosh, the second stage ignites and pulls away from the booster; all that would take one second.

For the first flight I was going to fly BB-shot with just the motors in the first stage. "Take it one step at a time" as Dad used to say. I ran the BB-Shot design through the HP computer program to check its stability. But something seemed wrong. My experience, my gut if you will, told me I had to add weight to the nose. But "the computer said" it was OK. And did I do the old-fashioned test of swinging the rocket around my head in a circle to see if it nosed into the wind? No. I believed the computer.

Author with BB-Shot rocket; 1983

I set the rocket on the pad, hooked it up, gave a countdown, and clicked the camera shutter as BB-Shot roared upward. Three feet above the launch rod it began a moderate turn. But then it tucked under and went head over teakettle and, fortunately, landed on its side in tall grass, smoldering; no damage!

The smell of sulfur from spent model rocket motors filled my bright red 1979 Honda Civic as I took BB-Shot home. There had to be a mistake somewhere in the computer program. I "played computer" by going through all the lines of code and following all the different paths just as the computer would. I had done this previously, but I must have missed something. In about an hour after "running" a few different logic paths I discovered the error. I made the change and reran the program the next day at work during lunch. My gut was right; I added a little lead in the nose to move the CG farther forward and flew BB-Shot Flight 2; it was a beautiful flight with all seven rockets firing.

Here was a terrific example of how I could *see* the effects of the equations on the result. Again I learned to trust my intuition despite what the computer said. If it looks wrong, it usually is. A computer is just a tool not an engineering god. And twenty years later when I was in program management I had to fight this "computer worship" every breathing minute. Not only for technical stuff, but for computer generated schedules, finance, you name it. The computer is only as good as its programmer (the garbage in, garbage out axiom).

A few weeks later BB-Shot flew with the upper stage live; a great flight. The flashbulb mercury switch staging worked; it ignited the three upper-stage motors and they all lit-off. The booster separated and its parachute came out and the upper stage went to about two thousand feet and was recovered successfully. What a day!

I wrote another paper, this one on flashbulb/mercury switch staging.

BB-shot successful flight; 1983

* * *

After years of design and building, I finally finished the space shuttle model around 1982 or '83. I had shown in-work photos to some of my Propulsion friends, and they all wanted to see this launch.

There was fanfare; Vic Petersen, a satellite attitude and control guy and a professional photographer, came out and snapped many photos and also devised a camera in a box mounted only inches from the shuttle to get a NASA-type shot at the base of the pad. There were video cameras too. And Joyce came to see this one after a several year hiatus from accompanying me to rocket launches.

Author with space shuttle model rocket
Courtesy of Vic Petersen

"Heads up; launch!" someone yelled. This meant, stop what you're doing and watch out, this thing could go anywhere!

"Five…four…three…two…one. Ignition!" It rose, but one solid rocket booster, SRB, remained on the pad. Oh, NOOOooo! The orbiter and tank and a single SRB flew up the rod and did a cartwheel. Meanwhile the lone SRB ignited as it was tipping over and flew like a mosquito on speed. The pin-wheeling shuttle fell on some dry grass and a small fire started. "FIRE! FIRE!" someone yelled as if it was a forest fire and they squirted about three tablespoons of water on it to put it out.

The only damage to the orbiter was a snapped off vertical tail; easy fix. But what about the solid rocket left behind on the pad? I designed a little clip that I'd made from a paperclip to hold the SRBs in place until they fired.

Two weeks later, the second flight, same crowd; a successful liftoff with all engines burning.

Liftoff of the author's space shuttle model
Courtesy of Vic Petersen

It left the rod but made a big, wide loop and at the top of the loop the SRBs fell off; the new clip design worked!

I collected the pieces and put them in the trunk of my car. The model was just too complex and I could see that it just wasn't going to fly correctly. Later, I discovered that the motors I used for the orbiter did not have the thrust that the manufacturer claimed, and modifications would be too extensive. So I "retired" the model.

But just after the shuttle model flight, I had a second act that day. A few years earlier I had built a model of the Saturn V. It was a highly modified version of a three-foot-tall kit that was supposed to fly with just one motor. I thought that looked silly. So I modified the kit to fly with five motors, as well as adding a second stage using the upper stage flashbulb ignition system that I had come up with.

I had flown it three times before and it was just spectacular. It would lift off and go straight up with a very slow roll. Then the second stage would ignite, with a flashbulb mercury switch staging system of course, and it would pull away from the booster climbing another five hundred feet or so. The recovery was three separate pieces: the booster, second stage, and the nose section. Each came down on multiple parachutes. It was just beautiful. But that was when no "fans" were watching.

The large, gleaming white Saturn rocket with black roll patterns stood majestically waiting for flight number four with my propulsion friends watching in angst: "Five...four...three...two...one. Ignition!" It began to rise, but right away I could see it was too slow. It cleared the six-foot rod and after about ten feet it slowly tumbled, finally landing on its side, then the mercury switch fired the flashbulb and the upper stage fired. It shot forward along the ground about a foot, then stopped in some tall grass. POP! The parachutes deployed on the ground. Not pretty. I picked up the remains (actually there was little damage to this one too), and with a sigh put those smoldering pieces in the trunk of my car to accompany the smoldering space shuttle model.

But, alas, I had a curtain call; it was a *big* F engine booster and E upper-stage that burned for four seconds. It had flown twice before—beautiful flights. "Five...four...three...two...one. Ignition!" A huge yellow flame erupted from the base of the rocket and then BLAM! The motor blew its guts out: the nozzle out one end and the propellant out the other. The upper stage, with the flashbulb assembly and sporting a very pointy nose cone, was blown clear of the booster and was tumbling head over heels about twenty feet above us. Pointy nose cone, tail; pointy nose cone, tail; which way would it fire? "Take cover!" someone yelled. Then, swooosh, it headed for the bay (fortunately) and burned for four very long seconds. I think it may have reached Fremont; well, not really.

Successful flight of author's Saturn V rocket

My friends brought me the booster remnants. One of my Lockheed friends said, "Not exactly a blue ribbon day, eh, Bill?"

28

I wanted to expand my boundaries from propulsion. It was time to move on. True, I could be a professional propulsion engineer, and that was intriguing, and I truly enjoyed the Propulsion group camaraderie, but my ambition was to lead an entire project and to learn more about satellites.

I wanted to join the System Engineering Department within Lockheed at Sunnyvale. These guys saw the whole vehicle and analyzed all mission phases.

I interviewed with Byron, a rather large man, always beet red; he was bald and had an unmistakable grunt. Byron agreed to let me work for him for six weeks and at the end of that time if I didn't like it I could go back to propulsion.

When I went to Byron's group, I was somewhat disappointed. I thought I'd do space vehicle level stuff but, alas, I was assigned to do requirements for ground support equipment (GSE). I tried to comfort myself by thinking of my model rocket experience years earlier when I decided on telephones for the tracker guys and realized how important GSE really was.

GSE is all the mechanical and electrical equipment and stuff needed to do the care and feeding of the spaceship before it launches. I surmised that if I learned that, then I'd end up learning all about the spacecraft.

I quickly got involved in satellite test and launch base operations by being one of a team of three to figure out the requirements for all of these pieces of equipment.

Since I had a propulsion background, I was assigned to determine the requirements for the new propellant loading carts. These were different in that this propulsion system used hypergolic propellants. The memory of Mr. Sampy mixing alcohol and acid in the high school chemistry lab hood saying, "Watch this!" came back to me.

My old gang in the propulsion group supplied the detailed propellant requirements. My job was to translate these into design requirements for the propellant loading GSE.

I made many trips to the Santa Maria area to discuss propellant loading logistics with the guys at the base. I was responsible for documenting not just propellant loading stuff, but *all* of the requirements of the satellite at the launch base from propellant to telephones and offices.

Over the several years I had already been working on satellites, I had found that tons of documents were written, signed off, and filed but very few were ever read. To prove this point I stuck in a requirement that said, "At the launching pad blockhouse, there shall be a constant supply of plain M&Ms for the Spacecraft Systems Engineer (me) during propellant loading operations." A few years later when I went to the base for the launch preparations, there was a huge jar of M&Ms and the Air Force captain, whom I knew very well, said, "Bill, I need you to sign here that the M&M requirement 3.1.3.4.1 (typical specification paragraph marking system) has been verified and is complete." We both laughed. He was the only one that caught it.

About two years later I was made supervisor and I hired John, a big lad from Nebraska. He worked for me while we were doing this GSE requirements stuff and he slipped in a phony requirement too (we collaborated). His was a requirement for a basketball court outside of the engineering building to be used by the guys during lunch. Same thing, "Hey, John and Bill, you guys need to sign off on something around back." We went through a few antiquated doors following the typical old-style green, gray, and white square-tiled floors. Exiting through the back door we went around the corner and there was a brand new asphalt basketball half court with lines and everything.

Turns out that, no, they did *not* do it because we told them to. Unbeknownst to us they were going to do this anyway for the technicians and it was already in their planning. When the captain saw the requirement he hooked them together as a gag. The folks at the base enjoyed our humor, but our Lockheed program management didn't; no laughing, this is serious stuff. And it was serious, but we are human too and we want to enjoy coming to work.

There was another document that John and I wrote. When there is a launch with many people going to the base, either the Cape or Vandenberg, or wherever, there are lots of logistics that engineers and others must follow. There's safety training, badging instructions, lodging, how to get your time card filled out, all kinds of things.

On a previous campaign, John and I were a little disgruntled when we discovered that the logistics document we wrote was read by no one. Surprise! We decided to make this one worth reading. We put in all kinds of funny things, and had a few folks do a test read and it got rave reviews. We sent it through the signature chain knowing that no one would read it. Well, we were wrong; our director read it (we think he was tipped off), and called John and me in and read us the riot act. Turns out the customer got a bootleg copy of it and absolutely loved it, but the management would not or could not see humor in a space program; heaven forbid.

* * *

One day Byron came to my desk, scanned my area with a funny look on his face, and then said, "Come to my office." I went into his office and he asked me why there were papers on my desk.

"What do you mean?"

"What do you mean, 'What do you mean?' Why are there papers on your desk?" I struggled for the meaning behind this as I scanned his desk. Nothing. Just a framed photograph, a few memorabilia, a time card, and a calendar.

"I'm working on my document."

"How many people do you have working for you?"

"Seven."

"And you don't think that with seven people they couldn't fit in one more document?"

"Well, this one I started before I became supervisor a few weeks ago and I thought I would—"

"No! Your job is to supervise. Your job is to be sure everyone is working and to keep track of their progress. Your desk should have not

133

one piece of paper on it. It's called delegation. This will take you some time to get used to, but you must. You have to let go."

"But—"

I'll give you two weeks to get yourself into this mode."

I left his office. First I had feelings of failure, but then I realized he had just given me a gift. He was teaching me how to lead. A few days later I asked one of my folks to complete my document and I started to learn to be supportive of their needs or to help with roadblocks. I found myself negotiating with other supervisors and sometimes managers on behalf of one of my folks. I was learning.

29

I **already knew most** of the guys at the launch base from my earlier propellant loading experiences. So in my new assignment, some of us were breaking ground with these hypergolic propellants. There were, however, lots of old-timers that had launched rockets in the '60s with this stuff. One of them was Tom Young.

Tom was a very friendly, outgoing, energetic soul who absolutely loved to launch satellites. He and I hit it off immediately and he became my mentor. Over the course of several years we spent a tremendous amount of time together either at Vandenberg or in Sunnyvale laying out the logistics for launching different satellites, or in bars after hours. It doesn't really matter what satellite. The planning, logistics, equipment, requirements, meetings, and process were about the same no matter what program you were on.

I learned a lot from Tom through the many stories he told of the Agena days. Lockheed built a space vehicle known as Agena in the early 1960s. Dozens of them were built and launched. These vehicles were used for both classified and unclassified missions as well as for one of the Gemini manned space missions. It was best known for the first spy satellite known as Corona, the officially declassified code name.

In the very early sixties the government came up with the idea of flying a satellite with a camera in it to photograph Soviet missile launch sites, harbors, whatever. They created a program called Discoverer, but it was really Corona. It took several attempts but it finally worked and later went on to be the first recovered spacecraft from orbit. A specially configured airplane snagged the film capsule while it descended on its parachute. The film was immediately sent to Washington, D.C. for analysis. This capsule, or bucket as it was referred to, is on display at the Air & Space Museum in Washington, D.C., with photos of the parachute recovery.

Tom told me a lot of the stories with respect to things that went wrong and why. Once we were in the Technical Service Building, or TSB, at one of the launch facilities and Tom told me how someone had screwed up an Agena mission. "Well, there was this mechanical device that set the pitch angle of the rocket during the final burn. It was set incorrectly, a few pegs in the down direction, so we basically drove the sucker into the ocean," he said with a big laugh. "They gave the guy three days off with no pay."

"Is that a career ender?"

"Nah, we were just learning and sometimes there were screw-ups."

"So this was the trial and error time, I guess."

"Yeah, and there were lots of trials and plenty of errors," Tom said.

"I guess the poor bastard that got the three days off feels pretty bad."

A voice about three desks away said, "Ah, that would be me, . . and, yeah, I felt bad about it."

"Oh…well, you don't look the worse for wear," I said trying to soften my blunder. Tom turned toward the large bay area reminiscent of my North American Rockwell years and in his untactful way yelled out to the sea of occupied desks, "Hey, who here has ever been given three days off without pay?" The majority of the hands went up. I reacted and Tom told me that it was common for the guys at the base. "Because this is where the rubber meets the road," he said.

He told me lots of humorous but very technical stories about people involved and things that happened over the course of several programs. But those were the pioneering years; mistakes were made, and the art of flying satellites *was* refined by trial and error. No, these weren't incompetent people, they were explorers; they made the mistakes and paid for their growing pains. If someone makes a small mistake on a report, an analysis or an order for bolts, no one notices. But satellite operations and launch base mistakes were highly visible, even the minutest.

Launches were frequent then; with one every two weeks, and these were the guys who got it done. They were the *real* rocket/satellite guys. They took risks; they had to. And they had courage, a lot of courage. I feel privileged to know them.

Tom encouraged me to continue my journey and to focus on how to get the job done. He said, "One day you'll be leading a launch, I just know it." With that, I was inspired to pursue satellite test and launch operations, and I began to pursue my goal to be one of the console guys and give the final "GO" to launch a space vehicle.

Tom was a rocket man but from a satellite perspective. He introduced me to key players at Vandenberg and we enjoyed planning several satellite program launches. We worked on one particular program putting in sixty-hour weeks for months. Tom was in his fifties, me in my thirties. One Thursday evening after a whole day of grueling meetings in Sunnyvale I asked Tom if he wanted to go have a drink. He looked at me and said, "No, I'm really tired. I think I'll just head on back to Santa Maria tonight." He did and a few days later they found Tom at his home sitting in his easy chair; he was gone.

The loss was so very painful for me and many others as well. Many drove from Sunnyvale to Santa Maria for his funeral. The man was so enthusiastic about what he did. He knew no barriers and he got things done. He didn't care what a person's job title or rank was; if he thought an idea was dumb he'd let them know. He wasn't a bully, not at all; he was a leader. I vowed to follow his passion, his execution of "common sense," and his enthusiasm. But I also learned, especially as years went by and others I'd known passed away, to try to enjoy life as best I could, not take this all too seriously, and most of all cherish those around you for they could be gone in a flash.

Someone once told me, Bill, if you're lying on your deathbed, do you really think you'll say, "Oh man, I wish I would have worked more overtime for the company"? I don't think so.

I think of Tom a lot. I can still hear him excitedly describing something or telling a really funny story. He is still painfully missed, by many.

* * *

I had overseen a few propellant loading operations and I came up with an idea to reduce the time it took to accomplish the loading. To make a change in aerospace, satellites anyway, you have to bring your presentation to a Change Control Board or CCB, sometimes called a Configuration Control Board. This board listens to the change and then makes sure that any stakeholders don't have a problem with it. If it's approved the change is documented and then drawings or procedures are changed and those affected documents must be itemized by the presenter. I had done many of these CCBs before and I was getting so I wasn't too nervous about them. The board was the program senior management. I prepared my charts for this change and got on the CCB meeting schedule. The following week I went to the conference room. I was with all the other presenters and their supporters. There were probably sixty people in the room. It was a small room for sixty people; it had a long table in the center for the board members. A white screen was at the front of the room and chairs lined the walls resting only a few feet from the larger, cushier rocking-type chairs at the table.

There was an unwritten rule: Only the board members sat at the table. And another rule was: the program manager always sat at the head of the table. Once some new kid came into the CCB for a presentation; being one of the first ones there he pulled out the chair at the head of the table and sat down. As people came in they sat around the room leaving him conspicuously at the head of the table. He was just getting up when Vance Coffman, program manager at the time but who went on to become the CEO of the entire company, came in. Someone said to the young man sitting at the head of the table, "Son, I think you'd better sit somewhere else."

"No," Vance said to the young man, "if you want to sit there that's fine; I'll sit over here." And he grabbed a seat along the wall. That was real class on Vance's part.

But on this day it was business as usual, with all of the management in their positions. Only the light reflected from the large screen bathed the room. I was first on the agenda and began my pitch. Halfway through I got a sinking feeling that I hadn't prepared the presentation all that well, but I was hoping I could wing it and get away with it. I concluded with my recommendation chart, the last chart; so far so good.

Silence. Then, Connie Chambers, the chief systems engineer of the program said, "Gentlemen, this presenter did not present any other options to his suggested change; he did not present the risks; he did not present a logical path to his conclusions, and I see nothing to support any clear advantage in doing this. I suggest that this presenter return next week with a more compelling argument." Murmur, murmur, then Vance said, "I agree, return next week, Bill. Next."

I left with my tail between my legs. It ruined my whole week. Although I knew there was a grain, OK two grains, of truth to it, it seemed somewhat harsh. A few people who weren't even at the meeting stopped by my desk and consoled me; they had heard about my roasting through the grapevine.

I revised my presentation and went to CCB the following week and bang, bang, bang I gave a very crisp, concise presentation. It passed. A few hours after that second CCB meeting, Connie Chambers called me into his office. He asked me to sit down and then he told me that he felt bad and wanted to talk to me about "it."

"Bill, the board got together a few weeks ago and we discussed the CCB meetings and we all agreed that the presentations were getting pretty sloppy; many were incomplete, and some were just plain poor. We decided to single out an individual and make an example of him or her so the word would get around. You signed up for that week and we all thought you could take the heat, so we nailed you to help the quality of everyone's presentations improve. The next week they were remarkable. So, sorry we used you, but again, we thought you could take it." He gave me a big grin and I stood, shook his hand, and mumbled something about him owing me a beer.

I didn't feel bad at all about being "used." I was flattered they picked me because they thought I could take it; and I did. I worked with Connie for several years after that. He was a tremendous leader and an excellent systems engineer. He could cut through all the bull and get to the bottom line. I watched this and tried to emulate his methods. To this day I acknowledge that it was Connie who helped me develop the ability to see the basic issue behind a complex problem, and to find a path forward by filtering all the analyses and charts and graphs. You have to be able to put it together, step back and see the bigger picture, and not lose sight of the goal; easy to say but difficult to do.

Connie helped me get that vision and many years later I got to where I could cut through a lot of bull to get to the real issue(s) and then have the experts solve the problem—but never as well as Connie. He passed away a few years after he retired. I still have the pamphlet from his memorial service on my desk to remind me of him and how lucky I was to know him and to watch him work. I will always miss him.

30

On the other hand, there are occasions where a little creativity can't hurt. Once we had to prepare cost estimates for a customer. We didn't have the normal six weeks or even one week to do this. All of the subsystems people had to conjure up quotes with their basis of estimates, and present everything to the customer (charts; lots of charts).

The ground segment manager got up and said his cost for this particular modification would be seven hundred thousand dollars. The customer hounded him with questions; he questioned all of his estimates and gave him ten action items.

My turn, space segment (spacecraft); I said, "After comparing this modification of the XYZ mod we did on the ABC program, the price will be $1,747,566.27."

Silence for a while, then "Thanks, Bill"; not another word. And I sat down. Sometimes you add just a little color to the number to at least make it look like you spent days coming up with the answer. In this case my real "P O squared A" (Pulled Out of Ass) estimate was $1,750,000. I liked the other number better. So did they.

* * *

There are these things called schedules. Schedules run everything. On one program I was on, they put all seventeen thousand line items into a scheduling computer program. The computer said that we would launch in seventeen years; so much for computers.

On another program we were the subcontractor reporting to a prime. In a small conference room they posted little stickies that spelled out interdependencies, lists of who owes what to whom and by when throughout the course of the program; these little notes were all over the walls but laid out in chronological order. These stickies were to be connected to other stickies to show the relationship between them. So they used colored yarn. Yes, yarn. There were about ten people in a conference room and they were stringing yarn. It looked like a room wearing a multicolored sweater. Yarn didn't work.

* * *

After doing ground support equipment and launch base operations for about five years I was offered the position of supervisor of Systems Engineering Vehicle Test. This was a very tough job. It was leading the teams that took the spacecraft through factory testing including all of the environments. The test organization worked for the test manager. I was supervisor of the systems engineers who derived test requirements, monitored these tests, tracked the test discrepancies, coordinated the troubleshooting when things didn't go well, and made presentations to the customer at program management reviews; I got to take all the credit for the hard work that the test crews did. Customers like guys with ties.

I agreed to take the assignment and I felt like I was thrown into a very deep lake tied to an anvil. Jim Roulo was my manager and Gerry Phelps was the test manager at the time. These two guys helped me and very patiently kept me in check. I received many phone calls at two or three in the morning from the test control center. "We had a gyro count failure; what should we do?"

"I don't know…do something else until morning," was my normal response. They finally stopped calling, I think they thought they had tormented the new guy enough.

Gerry used to call Jim Roulo at two a.m., and when Jim answered the phone, Gerry would say, "So what are you doing up?"

Every morning there was an eight o'clock meeting and the lead test conductor went over the engineering notes from the day and night before. They reviewed the tests that were going to be run that day, and we made plans for next day's testing. We did this every day; sometimes Christmas day. When things went wrong, especially if a box failed, I got anxious reactions, like it was my fault. This went on for about six months and finally it occurred to me that this was why we tested, to find out these things before we flew, not after; I decided not to take it personally. After that when someone would say a box failed, I'd first ask if it was a true failure or if we had screwed up and "smoked it." If they said it was a true failure I'd say, "GREAT!" We then took it to a failure review board (FRB) where the program management decided what to do. Watching that process for a few years was another brick in a very strong foundation that I had no idea was building beneath my feet.

I did this job for over a year and studied the decision making process. Gerry Phelps once said to me, "It's easy, you just keep them going." And that's true. You don't want an army of people just standing around because you or someone in management can't make up their mind about what to do. Let the test engineers or vehicle engineers make a recommendation, make a decision, and keep going. Many years later this "process" would become so bogged down with so many people who just *had* to be in the decision loop that test engineers turned into button pushers. And System Engineering, comprised mostly of people with no test or hardware experience (but who *had* to understand before they could make a decision) brought many test schedules to a standstill. The new, young college grads should not be assigned to Systems Engineering right out of college. They should first do engineering analyses, hardware or software development, or test. Only then can they have a chance of understanding what it takes to satisfy the system requirements, let alone how to write them.

* * *

I actually enjoyed being a supervisor. I didn't dread the performance reviews and dealing with the people part of the job, which to me was the entire job. I used to say, "We supervise and manage people, not things."

When there were arguments between employees I'd bring them both into Jim Roulo's office, which had a door, to hear both sides of the story. (Sometimes Jim was there; sometimes not.) I called them hearings. It's amazing how easily most of these arguments were quickly resolved by doing that.

The program I was on hit a real slowdown and sometime in 1994 charge numbers were getting slim and layoffs were already happening. I was at my rope's end with the bureaucracy, although it would get terribly worse years later after the Lockheed Martin merger, so I was ready for a change.

Vera Kilston, who I knew from a previous program and who had a fabulous sense of humor, came to my cubicle and said, "Hey, Bill, there's a new proposal for a commercial imaging satellite and they could really use your test experience to lay out the test program and write the proposal material. Besides, it'll get you outta here."

"Sounds like a plan to me; when do I start?"

"Let me talk to the folks and I'll get back to you, but we need you." This came right on the heels of completing the tests on a particular spacecraft, and the management had been asking us to try to find new work. This seemed like a good opportunity and I wouldn't have to be at an 8:00 a.m. meeting every day, at least not for a while.

I got the green light and went over there that Monday morning. It was a leased building and the whole team was in one area, not scattered around a huge building like most of the programs on the main campus. The name of the program was Commercial Remote Sensing System (CRSS), pronounced "Chris."

It was the whole enchilada, meaning it included the spacecraft and the ground stations. I went over and they had just come up with the spacecraft concept. Because this was a commercial fixed-price program we basically could do whatever we wanted. Well, almost.

31

This new program was to take images of the earth to one meter resolution and sell them commercially. One meter resolution meant that we were required to build a spaceship, actually two spaceships, which could photograph a coffee table on a front lawn from about 385 miles. Each spacecraft had to live seven years on-orbit and, oh by the way, we were to build not only the two spacecraft but also the ground stations to control the spacecraft around the globe, and to produce, store, print, and ship photos to customers.

A few months after I joined the all-Lockheed CRSS proposal, Space Imaging, Inc. was formed by Lockheed for this specific endeavor and they were now the customer.

My job was to lead the satellite integration, test and launch operations group and hire a staff of engineers and technicians to test and launch the two CRSS satellites. All we had were a few presentation charts. We had to start from scratch. I hired a few guys to be the leads of test engineering and electrical ground support equipment (GSE), Al Wietecha and Fred Reardon, respectively. They sat with me and we discussed philosophy. I had only a few demands about how I wanted some things to be done and they wholeheartedly agreed.

I hired nearly thirty-five people over a year and we had quite a team. I had to do management stuff, like personnel reviews every year and other things like that, but I really didn't mind those things. I enjoyed being a manager and I enjoyed letting the crew share in the responsibilities.

On other programs, the supervisors and managers signed everything. The only thing I signed on CRSS was the Spacecraft Test Plan and purchase orders over a thousand dollars. The leads signed off on the test procedures, operations orders, and such. For money, I gave them a budget of so much money per month to buy little stuff and it was their responsibility to manage it. That worked really well and gave them even more of a sense of ownership.

Earlier on the CRSS program it was just me doing the test stuff and I made a sketch of a satellite test control center for the proposal. I drew a sketch of a computer with magnetic tape reels mounted on it. A year or so later Doug Dorsett, one or two years out of college, came into my office with a puzzled look on his face and showed me a copy of that chart. He wanted to know if I was set on the magnetic tape data acquisition system like the ones we had used to record solid rockets data years before.

"Well, Doug, frankly, it's all I'm familiar with."

"What if I could find something a little more state of the art... ah, no offense," he said tapping his fingers together with a big smile on his face.

"None taken and I'm all ears."

"Give me an hour." And he left, quickly; whoosh. About an hour later he came back with Fred and Al in tow and showed what he'd gotten off the internet. It was a juke box arrangement that recorded tons of data on small cassette tapes (this was 1995, mind you, pretty state of the art then). He had prepared a presentation for me of the machine, how it would interface with a test system, the cost, how long for delivery, and estimates on the number of cassettes to record all of our data. And he did all of that in an hour. He said it would be fifteen thousand dollars.

I told him to buy two.

Afterward I brought in Al and Fred and discussed a plan I had and, with their agreement, I called Doug back into my office.

"Doug, do you think you can do the entire test system leveraging off of the ground station software?"

"Yeah!" he said tapping his fingers together really fast now. Whoosh! He was gone, then furiously typing out plans and coordinating the design of the entire test control center for our program; he was two years out of college.

* * *

145

We got through the preliminary design review (PDR), and Al and Fred and "the kids" did great. It was better than great; it was terrific. They had everything nailed. We brought over some of the guys from heritage programs and they looked at our computer system with pictures on the screen of a satellite and electrical circuit routings and antennas going back and forth. It was dynamite.

After the PDR I remember driving home feeling so full, satisfied, and proud. I reminisced a little about my wind tunnel testing and how my supervisor gave me a ton of responsibility and how I just loved that; and how my manager at UTC didn't entrust me and how I disliked that.

The critical design review came several months later and we showed how all of our stuff was designed and how our long lead equipment was getting built. The ground support equipment is done earlier that the spacecraft flight hardware because it has *got* to be there and working before the satellite arrives.

At the same time, we were working with the launch base guys. Actually they were the Lockheed guys stationed at Vandenberg Air Force Base (VAFB), whom I knew from several previous programs. I subcontracted them to load our propellant and transport the spacecraft. At the time they had no transporter except a huge transportation system that took about fifty people and a C-5 airplane to move. No thank you. And besides, our little satellite would have been like a pea-in-a-pickup with that thing.

The year before, just before PDR, I took a walk out to a back lot at Lockheed where they stored old hardware; it was basically a junk yard. An old white transporter was parked in the middle of the lot. I found someone with keys to get in. We opened the rear door on the trailer and peered in. It looked like with a little work we could use it. I contacted Gary Prestridge at VAFB and he sent his transportation guys up. I knew it was a satellite transporter for a previous program that they were long done with. Gary found out that the Air Force owned it and they said we could fix it up and use it.

I went to VAFB to discuss my idea of shipping the encapsulated spacecraft, our satellite inside the booster fairing (nose cone), in this transporter. They had driven it down to VAFB and assessed its condition after they got rid of all the spiders in it, on it, and under it. They said that with a little paint and some modifications it would work just fine.

I met their chief mechanical design engineer, Pete, and we discussed the tilting mechanism that would tilt the encapsulated spacecraft from vertical to horizontal while mounted to the transporter. I called it the "pizza pan" and the name stuck. But just before the meeting started, Pete asked, "Are you *the* Bill Dye?"

"What do you mean *the*?"

"Are you the Bill Dye that wrote those model rocket papers on oil flow visualization and flashbulb staging?"

"Why, yes; you remember those? You must be a model rocket guy."

"Those were landmark papers."

Frankly, I was surprised. I truly didn't think they would be "landmark," let alone remembered by anyone. I had to sleep with two pillows that night my head was so big. But I got over it pretty quickly.

* * *

Encapsulating the spacecraft with the booster fairing while still in the Sunnyvale high bay would allow us to use the fairing as a shipping cover to protect the sensitive optics as well as eliminating a processing facility at the base. In other words, since the spacecraft would be encapsulated, that meant it could be shipped directly to the launching pad, thus skipping the processing facility where one normally checks out the spacecraft, loads propellants, and encapsulates.

The encapsulated spacecraft would be stacked directly to the booster, hooked up, checked out, fueled, and ready to go. Simple and cheaper.

One difficulty was how to get the fairing around the spacecraft without damaging anything like antennas, solar panels, or sensors. I sketched a concept and gave it to Marty Hanson and his mechanical GSE guys, and years later I saw what I sketched come to be. That's a pretty good feeling seeing something that you conceived in operation. And, it worked fine.

* * *

Working with "the kids" was a lot of fun. This program was small and everyone knew each other. Since I was the spacecraft assembly, test and launch operations (ATLO) manager, I took special interest in the training of the test crew as well as our test supervisors. There are certain very subtle signs you see that reflect the morale and the dedication of the crew. One was while the spacecraft was in test about a year before launch. We were in the midst of weeding out the myriad of start-up problems like wrong database values in the computer that made the temperature monitors indicate one million degrees; or difficulties with the encryption/description of the commands and telemetry to and from the spacecraft.

Every morning at 7:30 I held a test meeting in a conference room very close to the high bay. The test engineer read the test conductor's log to the attendees describing what tests had been conducted the day before and if there were any issues or discrepancies. After that, there was another test engineer (day shift) that read what the plan was for the day. We reviewed if there were any mechanical operations on the vehicle that would require the spacecraft to be powered off. Did we have a full crew (anyone sick)? Were there any issues with the ground support equipment? Were we going to do any troubleshooting on the vehicle to track down a previously discovered problem? All these were planned out at this meeting every morning.

I arrived at the conference room a little earlier than usual, about 7:10 a.m., for our daily test meeting so I thought I'd be the first one there. But sleeping on the conference table was Tommy Romano, one of the young test engineers. I woke him up and he crawled off the table very sleepy-eyed. He said he'd been called in around midnight to troubleshoot a problem with commanding. The test crew on duty seemed to have gotten the spacecraft into a strange state and it got "locked up." It took him until around 4:30 a.m. to diagnose and then fix the problem. He decided to just curl up on the table rather than go home.

This was the critical sign; this showed me just one example of the dedication of these people. It was *our* spacecraft, not mine. I felt myself relax, and at that moment I knew this program would be a success because Tommy was curled up on the table.

These guys were up all hours of the night every day of the week to get the spacecraft tested. Occasionally I brought in pizzas to the test control center in the evening or at lunch. Another long night was reported and I asked if they'd had anything to eat. Tommy said they all had pizza. "The stuff I bought a week ago?"

"Yeah, it was fine!"

Dedication is eating week-old pizza rather than take the time to go out and buy more.

However, one must be ever vigilant for the times when "the kids" might be getting a tad cocky. It's a fine line between fanning the enthusiasm flames and creating a monster. The flight computer on the spacecraft had what is called EEPROM, pronounced "double E Prom." It's **E**lectrically **E**rasable **P**rogrammable **R**ead-**O**nly **M**emory. This EEPROM was the heart of our safe mode, which would point the spacecraft into the sun should something go wrong with the primary computer.

The code that ran this was burned in; that is, typed in manually; it was a somewhat dangerous task because even though the word "erasable" was in the description of this memory, there were times when that wasn't the case. Any mistake in loading the code could mean we would have to take the box off the spacecraft and send it back to BAE, the manufacturer of the EEPROM card, and have it reset. This cycle took about three weeks before it got back to us. And this would make me, as well as management, *very* unhappy.

Bill Clouse was the flight software engineer and virtually singlehandedly got the code running after unsuccessful attempts by others before him. While we were in the early stages of vehicle test, we discovered a problem in the safe mode code within the EEPROM. It had to be reprogrammed directly on the spacecraft and I asked Bill to do it. He asked for Tommy Romano to be the test conductor since he was most familiar with the vehicle processor.

Bill and Tommy started the process of recoding the EEPROM. Bill would read from his prepared and pretested script of commands, one command at a time. Tommy would read it back; Bill would concur and then Tommy would hit "send" to send the command to the vehicle and thus burn it into the EEPROM.

This went on for a good twenty minutes and Tommy was becoming just a bit cavalier in hitting the send button just a smidge too fast for Bill. Bill said, "OK, next is…" and then read him the command. Tommy read it back and hit "send."

Bill quickly said, "But, *before* you hit send … "

Tommy's eyes grew to saucers.

"Gotcha," Billy said.

"You bastard!" Tommy said. And his rapid sending ceased.

* * *

Doug ordered a few servers for the storing of test data. These were quite big and came in a box about the size of a refrigerator. One of the boxes was in the conference room.

Prior to one of our major design reviews about a year earlier, I insisted that the electrical connectors that connect to the spacecraft be such that it would be impossible to hook up the connectors incorrectly. Andy Coughlin, the electrical GSE engineer, assured me that this was so. Several months later we were powering on the spacecraft after it was down for several days for mechanical operations. I was told the night before that Andy nearly smoked the bird by hooking up two GSE connectors the wrong way. I was pretty angry, but I had an evening to calm down and to find out what happened; but I suspected Andy just screwed up.

I arrived at the morning meeting early, waiting to skin Andy. I saw the large server box sitting in the corner and asked Doug if he wanted the box. He didn't, so I asked him to help me modify it. And we did.

Everyone started to file into the conference room for the 7:30 a.m. meeting and Andy slid into his spot at the table hiding his eyes from me. The test conductor read the notes from the previous day and seemingly breezed through the incident with, "The vehicle was powered on at 1755 but was reconfigured and power was reapplied at 1830. The first test was a gyro earth rate…" I waited. One Mississippi, two Mississippi … nothing. Then I said, "Just one freaking moment, could someone please 'splain to me why we had to 'reconfigure' after the first power-on attempt?"

Willy, the test engineer reading the notes, said, "Ahhhhhhh, well, ahhhh, there was, ahhhh …"

Finally Andy spoke up and said, "I hooked up two GSE connectors incorrectly."

"Really. You mean the connectors that someone named Andy told me that hooking them up incorrectly could never happen?"

"Yes …"

"The Andy who assured me that all the connectors were either different or keyed differently?"

"Yes …"

"Well, there is only one thing to do…Andy, I find you guilty of not doing what you said you were going to do and for nearly smoking the spaceship; I hereby sentence you to ten minutes in test engineer's jail."

Doug opened the server cardboard door we made into a jail by putting bars on the box with a magic marker and cutting out a door. As the door opened all could see the "Test Engineer's Jail" sign we'd put in earlier. Andy got up, walked into the box, and Doug closed the door. The meeting continued for another ten minutes with lots of smiles. We were wrapping up and we heard Andy say, "Can I come out now?"

"No, two more minutes," I said. Then we heard a very low "OoooK."

I got my point across. Andy fixed the connectors so that could never happen again. And, yes, we did the due diligence to verify that no harm came to the spacecraft.

32

I was promoted a few months later from test manager to CRSS space segment manager; the previous manager retired. This meant that I was responsible for the entire spacecraft; both of them. Al took over as the manager of ATLO.

It took several months for me to get over the intense anxiety of this new position. I had to make many decisions daily. I learned very quickly to rely on the people that worked for me and to have them present me with options and their recommendations. Usually I agreed with what they recommended but it wasn't unusual for me to counter for reasons having to do with cost, schedule, or risk. The technical guys tell you what is best technically, but management has to integrate these other factors into the decision.

It was difficult being at the head of the table, being in "the fish bowl" as I called it, every breathing moment. But after about nine months I enjoyed it. I started to think I knew what I was doing and Tom Dougherty, the program manager and my boss, and others taught me well.

But I was mindful of not abusing this power. I could see how several other managers I'd known over twenty years took advantage of their position. Absolute power corrupts absolutely. It is so true. I kept thinking how I would like to be treated. Although, admittedly, I have had my moments where I would lose my temper and rip someone a new ass but usually they deserved it. Usually it was because they lied about something. I would not tolerate anyone lying to me just to cover their ass, or for any reason for that matter. I had to know that I could trust the people that worked for me. If they lied, how could I trust anything they said or recommended?

We completed all of the environmental testing; thermal vacuum testing that simulates space and demonstrates that everything will work in a space environment, as well as acoustic test where the spacecraft is subjected to noise levels to simulate the booster ascent vibration. We were three weeks from shipping it to the launch base. One of the last tests that we did was a test of the gyros. We conducted the test and a key parameter showed a significant drop. We spent a few days trying to decide if it was an error in the instrumentation, the test system, whatever. Nope, it was genuine.

The program came to a screeching halt. There was a problem with the fundamental design of this particular type of gyro. The design fault was extremely complicated and there was a lot of physics involved to "make it go." Tom brought in all kinds of physicists and scientists to help come up with a solution to the problem.

The investigation went on for months; meanwhile we started testing the second vehicle so we weren't just sitting around reading Superman comic books. For the gyros, it boiled down to this: there were about five different phenomena going on with this one symptom. The scientists could figure out about two or three of them, but could not guarantee that fixes for those two or three would totally fix the problem. They said that the gyros would only work for about six months before they died.

Space Imaging Company management, knowing that the gyros would last only six months, suggested that we put an extra gyro on the first vehicle. They made a business decision. Space Imaging wanted to be first to market with a commercial high-resolution photo of the earth from low earth orbit. They were willing to launch the first vehicle knowing full well that it would only last about a year and a half instead of the seven-year requirement.

I suggested putting a separate type of gyro on vehicle two. That plan was adopted and we were given the green light to proceed to modify the first vehicle, and then not long afterward for shipping the spacecraft.

But wait. We had a GPS receiver that was frankly...crap. Earlier in my new position as space segment manager I was concerned about this troublesome GPS receiver and I went on several trips to the subcontractor with the responsible equipment engineer to get up to speed on this thing and see if I could help get this box through its testing.

Author with CRSS spacecraft; 1999
Courtesy of Lockheed Martin; photograph by Doug Hart

In the lab the box was hooked up to many wires, coax cables, and oscilloscopes; all kinds of stuff. On the spacecraft, it's just a box hooked up to a coax cable that goes to an antenna and another connector for power and data. That's it.

Now, only weeks before we were to ship the bird to the base, I and a few others in the CRSS management were interviewing all the subsystem engineers to be sure all the testing had been done, all of the paper closed, and that we were ready to fly. During one of these meetings, I asked the communication subsystem guys if they had done a test of the GPS box in the flight configuration. They said they had done the box acceptance testing just like I saw it in the lab, with all of the wires.

So I asked them again, "Why didn't we do a flight configuration test by taking this box out into the parking lot and mounting a flight antenna on a broom stick and connecting the flight antenna to the box with the same type and length of cable that we are going to use on the spacecraft?"

"Well, the previous program administration was concerned that the box would get dirty if they took it outside. And the analysis says that it will be OK."

"But it's a sealed box and boxes can be cleaned, right? And, excuse me, but one test is worth a thousand analyses," I said.

I directed them to conduct the test—fast. I called it The Parking Lot Test. They flew down to Orange County, California, and did the test.

The test failed. It turned out that the receiver was so sensitive that the signals from the GPS satellites were overpowering the receiver and it basically didn't function. In short, the GPS satellite volume was too loud for the receiver and the receiver plugged its ears. This would have been a mission-ender. Without the GPS the location accuracy of the images would have been compromised.

What to do? We had a Failure Review Board and the communications engineers proposed putting in attenuation pads, little doo-hickys that reduced the signal going into the receiver. They put them in the parking lot test setup and it worked. It took a tech a day to put in a few of these things on the vehicle. *Now* we were just about ready to fly.

* * *

About nine months before the launch we practiced the encapsulation and transportation operations. The booster guys had shipped the fairing to us and they used our high bay as their storage site, so it was a win-win for them too. One night I had a dream that the fairing didn't separate from the Athena booster and the first IKONOS satellite never made it to orbit, or "went into the drink" as we say. It was vivid; I'd had those kinds of dreams before and most came to pass. But this was something I didn't want to boast about. I did tell the booster "Mission Manager" that there might be something wrong with the fairing, but I couldn't put my finger on just what that might be, so I didn't push it.

I had the dream again, two months before launch. No one cared when I said to look hard at the fairing design. I would go inside the fairing and just look at it, trying to figure out where there might be a design flaw.

33

Vandenberg Air Force Base Space Launch Complex 6 or SLC-6 (pronounced slick-6) was to be the launching pad for the space shuttle with DOD missions—called Blue Shuttles. Well, not really blue, but Air Force shuttles, so they called them blue. I bet they'd have found a blue dye for the tiles so they could have been blue though.

While building the "slick," they came across an Indian burial ground. This was around 1979 or 1980 when there wasn't much "political correctness." The Indians wanted time to evaluate the dig site to see if the Air Force should either continue, wait, or dig somewhere else altogether, as in move the launching pad.

The guys with lots of metal thingies on their uniform were not going to let this delay a critical national security project, so they overruled the waiting and, in the interest of national defense, continued to build the SLC-6 launch facility. (I'm sure there's another side to the story but let's just say the result was interpreted as such.) This made for, as Elmer Fud would say, "wear-we wear we unhappy Indy-wins," so the Indians put a curse on the pad! Nothing personal; just that anything launched from SLC-6 would fail, one way or another.

A few years later Challenger blew up shortly after launch at Kennedy (different launch facility so unrelated to the curse) and the DOD payload sponsors couldn't get off the shuttle manifest quick enough.

The pad was abandoned just as it was nearly completed. For about twenty years the pad was an empty shell. Stripped of huge electrical connectors, equipment and urinals (really) to be used somewhere else. Lockheed Martin was able to acquire the use of the pad and built a launching mount for our launch vehicle, the Athena rocket; on the cursed pad!

* * *

I had one guy, Doug Hart, responsible for all launch base operations. Dougie took the place of about 150 people on other, albeit much larger, programs.

Al, Fred, Marty and about fifteen test guys came down too; and that was it. No tons of managers, no systems engineering, no QA guys, no planners, no schedulers. Twenty guys tops, including me (Al and I were the only managers there).

The customer changed the name of our program and spacecraft from Commercial Remote Sensing System (CRSS) to IKONOS (eye-koh'-noce). The big day finally came when the IKONOS-1 testing was completed and we were ready to encapsulate the bird and ship it to the base.

Author inspecting encapsulation guide system
Courtesy of Lockheed Martin; photograph by Doug Hart

We loaded the satellite that was encapsulated by the flight fairing onto our shiny white transporter. The pizza pan support holding the assembly was tilted so it lay horizontally in the transporter. The lid was lifted and put into place.

The next day we drove it from Sunnyvale to Vandenberg. It took about seven hours with stops for food and bathroom breaks. As the big truck pulled up to the huge SLC-6 pad, our precious satellite looked pretty small.

The gleaming white nose cone tilted out of the transporter right at the base of the launching pad. We were all getting excited.

The encapsulated IKONOS spacecraft at the base of the pad
Courtesy of Lockheed Martin; photograph by Alan Surgi

The next day they lifted the fairing, with our spacecraft inside, off of the transporter pizza pan to the top of the booster where it was mated and bolted in place. Andy and the technicians (three of them—that's all we had) hooked up the booster to the spacecraft electrical connectors and we powered on the bird. The test engineers ran the launch base tests that we had practiced several times before, and in forty-five minutes we were done with satellite test. Now we waited…for two weeks. I marveled at how simple this launch was; it was the simplest I'd ever been on. I like to think I had a lot to do with that. Even the Athena booster guys had the keep-it-simple approach and their crew wasn't much bigger than ours.

Knowing that the SLC-6 launch facility was indeed cursed we just had to do something about it. I mean, how could we even think of launching our precious IKONOS satellite with even a smidge of a chance that the booster would "dunk it" due to a curse! Mind you now, all concerned knew very well about the curse. When I arrived at the launch base I was amused when I saw a bunch of very conservative engineers, who would deny any belief in ESP, psychic phenomena, paranormal stuff, with four-leaf clovers, good luck charms, and rabbits' feet; some had them all.

We formed a couple of "spirit cleansing" séances to disperse the curse. The SLC-6 Mobile Service Tower was very creepy—would've been even without knowledge of the curse. The day we arrived with the spacecraft in the transporter we wanted a guard posted, so two guys volunteered to stay overnight. The next morning as they left they said, "Never again." They reported strange noises all night, lights going on and off in sequence, and other odd occurrences.

Meanwhile, back in Sunnyvale, Mike Genzmer, a fellow I knew on the program, was able to make contact with the chief of the local tribe; he was trying to negotiate a deal to lift the curse for us, just for this one time. I never heard from him so I didn't know if he had succeeded or not. Since we didn't know if he could get them to remove the curse we decided to try ourselves.

One late afternoon four of us, one by one, made up an excuse to go to the pad. We exchanged our badges at the guard shack for pad badges (so if there's an accident, they might have a clue as to whose charred remains were still in the wreckage) and drove onto the pad deck. I parked the car and opened the car doors only to be greeted by the standard 40 knot, very cold Vandenberg spring wind. We made our way to (what was to have been) the shuttle assembly building (SAB), a huge building that mated with the mobile service tower (MST).

The Athena rocket with our satellite inside stood before us. We went up the rusty stairs (which we'd been told to keep off of) and found a level that seemed right. We squatted down in a circle (floor was filthy) and held hands (really) and conducted our ceremony. We had no idea what we were doing. But we all felt that there are things in this universe that even engineers can't explain. All through our little ceremony the wind died to nothing. But, when we finished, it returned. We all felt better.

* * *

In the launch control trailer, the place where the guys sit that really launch the rocket and power up the satellite, I noticed a joystick sitting on Dave's console. He was the booster launch conductor.

"What's that for, Dave?" I asked.

"Oh, that's our joystick. When tours come in they ask what that is and I tell them that if the rocket doesn't follow its flight path down range I switch to "manual" and fly it down range with the joystick." We all laughed.

"We had a group of foreigners come through," he continued. "One guy asked about it and I gave my stock answer. Five guys pulled out their pens and paper notebooks and wrote it down. I never told them it was a joke; I think they would have been too embarrassed."

Before we all went to VAFB for the launch campaign I celebrated my fiftieth birthday and had a party. Tom Fanshier, our electrical subsystem engineer, gave me a plain gray baseball cap with a ponytail attached to it as a gag gift. This to aid one that is "hair-challenged." I took it with me to the base because a couple of the booster guys had real ponytails.

About a week before the launch, Dave, the booster launch conductor, said, "You don't have the balls to wear that on-console on launch day."

"I'll tell you what. I'll wear it if you somehow add "joystick" into the countdown over the communication net on the day of the launch during the final countdown."

161

"Deal."

My very good friends, the Lockheed Vandenberg propellant guys, fueled the bird right on the launching pad, perfectly. My launch readiness presentation was one chart and we got the okey-dokey to launch from the customer, executives, and base commander. And we waited some more.

Finally the day before the launch, T-13 hours, about 8:00 p.m., the countdown started. I went to the launch trailer. We powered on the spacecraft just like it had been done three hundred times before in Sunnyvale when we tested the satellite. Now all we had to do was keep an eye on the spacecraft battery and wait until launch.

It was around 10:00 p.m. and everything looked OK. The night crew was set up and Fred and Al said they were going to leave in a few minutes. I turned and grabbed the trailer door knob when all of a sudden I heard, "What the hell happened? Where's the telemetry?"

I stopped and came back over to the test console. The screen was frozen. The fiberoptic link between the computers in the trailer and the GSE at the launching pad three miles away was not working properly. Fred Reardon and Andy Coughlin went to work. The drawings came out. Suddenly the telemetry came back on, then went off again. I told Fred it seemed to me like it was something that was heating up that might open a circuit. This was my big contribution to the effort.

Fred and Andy changed out a piece of fiberoptic equipment at the pad. It didn't fix the problem. Meanwhile I was quizzing our battery guy to find out if the batteries, which were pressure vessels, were happy.

Andy and Fred were looking pretty haggard. On the table was a huge ashtray full of cigarette butts; next to it were system manuals and drawings strewn everywhere. "I can't figure this damn thing out," Fred said. Al was there too and he kept saying, "This doesn't look good!" And these guys were the best.

The launch was around 11:30 a.m.; it was 5:00 a.m.; we were running out of time and Fred was running out of ideas. I knew we had only a few hours until we would abort the launch. Charlie, the launch director, came into the trailer at around 6:00 a.m. and asked me if we were "go."

"Hell yes, we're go!" I said, more calmly than I would have only moments before.

"Uh-huh, yeah, sure," he said as he looked at the computer system with yellow cables all over the floor.

"Trust me, Charlie, this is something really simple. They just have to find it." I told him to cover for me on the console. All I had to do was say "go" every half hour or so. I didn't think they would miss me for an hour or so.

A booster technician came in at 6:30 a.m. with his lunch pail in hand. He was just coming in for the shift change at seven. Fred told him what was going on and he said, "Hey, I have a complete spare fiberoptic system of ours that we use on the booster. Ya wanna try using that?"

"Shit yeah," Fred said and he, Andy and Mark Keyzer, the technician, went to work. They swapped it out in forty-five minutes. And Doug Dorsett, with deliberate but lightning speed, hooked up about ten or fifteen yellow cables to the patch panel on the front of the computer server. No procedures, no checklist; he just did it with knowledge, talent, and confidence.

Doug said he was ready. Andy called from the pad and said they were too. Fred said, "Fire this pig up!"—"pig" is an affectionate term—and on it came. And it stayed on; problem solved. It was a power supply that would get hot, shut off, cool down, turn on, then off. It was the only spare part we hadn't brought; Murphy strikes again.

The VAFB payload communications channel was connected to Space Imaging in Thornton (just north of Denver) and Jim Ellis was on the other end. More bad news; all three tracking stations were down. I asked the Thornton guys over this comm channel if Dave Flournoy, my spacecraft communications subsystem guy, was there. I heard Dave speak up (they were on a speaker phone). "Yes, I'm here, Bill."

"Dave, I know you RF guys; I'd be willing to bet that someone twiddled knobs and flipped switches to make something that was working just fine work better and now it's mis-configured. Would you get with each one and see if they have a switch in the wrong position or something?"

"Sure, will do." Dave left the Thornton conference room and started calling these RF guys in Alaska, Sweden, and Oklahoma.

T-1 hour.

I was SLD, satellite launch director. We went thought the T-1 hour check, "SLD-GO," I said when it was my turn. The weather officer indicated that the winds at the pad were 28 knots and the limit was 35 knots…and the speed was increasing. Great! But there was nothing we could do about that.

At T-40 minutes I looked at the booster guy with his real ponytail and said, "Whadda ya think? Now?"

"Yeah, let's do it."

We both turned around and donned our caps, mine with a ponytail. We sat right in front of the VIP section. You know, the separate glassed-in seating area. Joyce was there. So were the mucky-mucks. They all laughed.

I got on the launch comm net and said, "POC, this is SLD. The H – A – T is enabled and in place; check item 13b." The booster guys shrugged their shoulders as if to say, "Whaz zat?" Doug Hart pointed to his head and mouthed H, A, T and they all cracked up. I had upheld my side of the bargain with Dave, the launch conductor.

T-30 minutes, "SLD – GO." People's palms were sweating. I was nervous but mostly from the excitement of anticipating the launch, not from anxiety. I told myself things like: It's just another day. The roach-coach will be out in front of Building 150 in Sunnyvale in about thirty minutes. Just like any other day. There's nothing I can do to affect this one way or another. We've done everything we can do; now we just wait.

T-20 minutes. The final status and polling was to take place soon. Jim Ellis called me on the phone and said they were "go" because Dave Flournoy had talked to all three tracking stations and gotten them back online.

T-18 minutes. Final status. Charlie, the launch director (LD), called Dave, the launch conductor (LC). "LC, this is LD. What is your final status?"

"LD this is LC; inertial guidance is online, power to internal, destruct system is armed, *joystick enabled*, check item 12.1"

HE DID IT! He put in "joystick."

"This is the launch director. T-3 minutes. Final status call."

"Range?…GO All clear to launch."

"Safety?…"GO."

"Booster?…LC GO."

"Spacecraf?…SLD GO."

"Commander?...GO."

T-1 minute. The wind was really picking up. It was at 30 knots.

"T-37 seconds; hydraulics activated."

"Three...two...one. Liftoff of the Athena two rocket carrying Space Imaging's IKONOS spacecraft changing the way we look at the world. GO ATHENA! GO IKONOS!" the announcer said, or something really corny like that. Why do they do that? It's just embarrassing and sounds a bit too rah-rah for me. I wish they would just be quiet and let us listen to the normal comm net.

Liftoff of IKONOS, the first high-resolution commercial imaging satellite in space; September 24, 1999
Courtesy of Lockheed Martin; photograph by Russ Underwood

34

On a monitor directly in front of me I watched the Athena rise. We were several miles away so it took several seconds before we heard the crackle of the rocket motor. The airborne camera picked it up and followed it down range. The first stage burned out and the second stage ignited.

It flew out of sight. In several minutes it would be over the South Pole station and they would see the telemetry coming from the rocket. I noticed that the booster guys were huddled together looking at data. It was time for the South Pole contact. I heard Charlie ask if they had telemetry and they said, "No!"

One of the booster guys came over and said, "I wouldn't worry just yet; they could be off by just a few degrees with their antenna." Bull. This thing was radiating S band and a pigeon with an aluminum foil antenna would be able to hear it. Next station was Indie. Nothing. Finally, the program manager of the Athena came over to me and said they thought they'd they lost it and would we please come into the conference room. I let Jim, in Thornton, know what was going on and I went off the net and into the conference room.

We sat at this large table and the program manager asked his people what the data said. The flight dynamics guy said, "The booster first and second stage chamber pressures were right on the money, but it looks like the second stage was pushing extra weight uphill."

"How much weight?" I asked.

"About fourteen hundred pounds" I waited, waited some more, crickets ... OK, I guess I'll ask. "And how much does the fairing weigh?"

"Fourteen hundred pounds," someone said in a very low tone.

"Can this rocket make it into orbit with that amount of extra weight?"

"No," someone said.

I got up and started for the door, then turned and said, "I've got to tell them to stop looking for it; by now it's in the water."

I went back into the control center and got on the net. "Jim, they don't want to admit it yet, but the fairing didn't come off; it's in the water. It's over. Call off your search.

"Okay, thanks," he said very dejectedly. Tom Dougherty kept NORAD looking for it for another three hours and finally gave up.

Good thing Joyce was there. Several years earlier she had earned her master's degree from Santa Clara University. She then worked the required thousands of hours at post graduate internships before becoming a licensed marriage and family therapist.

There were mixed reactions. Some got angry, several guys cried, some withdrew, and some just talked and drank. She likened this to the loss of a newborn child. She said, "You spend all this time getting ready for this new life, for the birth, and then—just like that—it's gone." What a perfect analogy. To this day I wouldn't wish this experience on even our fiercest competitor.

There was an investigation. I wasn't on the official board but I went to the meetings. It was a connector inside the fairing that disconnected too soon, pulling the electrical contact that completed the fairing separation sequence.

Someone came out with "the first photo from IKONOS" and circulated it on the corporate web. It was a picture of a fish. It was brutal but really funny. We just had to start laughing again.

I waited a day or so for everyone to get back to Sunnyvale and held an all-hands meeting; I mentioned Joyce's analogy to the loss of a newborn child, but pointed out that we were somewhat fortunate in that we had a second bird; we had another chance. I knew they would follow my lead so I had to instill hope and tried my best to rally them.

IKONOS-2 had already been through its ambient functional test and so we started preparing it for thermal vac. Funny how we got no pressure from management but everyone busted their butts to get this thing tested carefully, but as quickly as possible, to get it to the base.

Four and a half months later we shipped IKONOS-2 to the base.

We were, however, even more concerned about the curse on the SLC-6 pad. IKONOS-2 arrived two weeks before launch and we had lots of time waiting for the booster guys to do their thing.

This time Mike Genzmer, the guy who was trying to contact the Indians, requested that a tour be allowed to see the pad and the rocket. Since this was a commercial launch, we had been giving tours all week so this was not an unusual request; right up until he said that no one could escort them on the pad. That would be a little more difficult. I made the arrangements for the tour to occur at 5:30 p.m. when just about everyone had gone home. I told the pad guard to expect this tour and that there would be a tour guide, Mike.

Mike hadn't been successful in arranging this tour for the first launch, but was able to pull it off for our second try. The tour was a group of American Indians, the guys that had put the curse on the pad in the first place, and they agreed to do a ceremony at the pad. The only stipulation was that no non-Indian persons were allowed to witness this ceremony. I trusted Mike and he trusted them. Mike ushered them around and in back of the MST. There was absolutely nothing near or connected to either the booster or the satellite back there; maybe some trash cans. He returned to the front of the complex, out of sight, and waited for them.

I went into Lompoc, the town just outside of the base, and had dinner. A little later I got a call and was told that they were done; they had left the base. They lifted the curse.

* * *

The second launch occurred on September 24 around 11:30 a.m., but this time the pad was socked in with fog. And once again I sat at the consol and said, "SLD – GO!" But we didn't fool with the ponytails and joystick; we thought that may have jinxed the first launch. We were all pretty superstitious by this time.

The liftoff was right on time, but no one celebrated until we heard the status of the IKONOS spacecraft. About fifteen minutes after launch, IKONOS looped around the South Pole. The Antarctica station reported hearing the booster transmitter. We knew the bird was in orbit, but was it in one piece? Things were looking good so far. After Antarctica it went around the world toward the North Pole and then over the Space Imaging Alaska station. Telemetry from IKONOS was relayed to the Thornton, Colorado Ground Station and it was from there that Jim Ellis announced, "We see telemetry, the solar panels are all deployed, it's sun pointing, and everything looks fine!" We were flying! Cheers rang out throughout the control room. We did it!

Within three hours we were all celebrating. We threw each other into the pool with our ties on. Phil Walker, the Eastman Kodak program manager who supplied the IKONOS imaging camera, took a photo of us in the pool. For me, it is a photo of my pinnacle: I had reached my goal; I was a console guy. What else could I do to come close to this feeling? We all knew that this program was unusual and we just happened to be at the right place and the right time to be able to do what we did. It would never happen again. And, unfortunately, that was true. Sometimes you just luck out and get on a program that's fun to work on and very rewarding.

The pinnacle! (L to R back) Dave Lebel, Bill Dye, Ed Irvin, Al Wietecha; (L to R front) Barbara Plante, Mark Keyzer, Doug Hart, Fred Reardon
Courtesy of Phil Walker

My parents watched the launch on the internet. They were thrilled. Later I played them a video of the launch countdown, with me in it!

For a few months before the IKONOS launch, Tom Dougherty would say, "Get ready," referring to the fact that he wanted me to be the program manager after launch. His job was to get it launched successfully and then turn it over to me. I would then be responsible for selling off the satellite to Space Imaging after we completed a myriad of on-orbit tests and resolved any bugs in the system.

Three days after launch, Tom said, "I've been made vice president and it's all yours now! Good-bye and good luck!" And away he went.

I had mixed emotions. I enjoyed working for Tom very much, learned a lot from him and would miss his leadership and his laughter; on the other hand, for the first time, I would be a program manager.

35

Two days after launch I was the new program manager of the IKONOS program. No pressure, no anxiety. With IKONOS successfully on orbit, my first task was to go to the ground station and "take command." I arrived at Space Imaging Inc. in Thornton, Colorado, the second day after launch. I walked into the conference room and there were about thirty people there. All eyes turned to me.

"Hey, terrific. The program manager is here; *he* can make the decision," someone said.

"What decision?"

"Well, the attitude and control system won't go into "fine" mode. We know it's because the coefficients need to be tweaked and we know how much. But we're not sure we want to risk up-linking those numbers; what if it breaks something?" I looked at Bill Clouse, head of the flight software, a software genius and my good friend. He very covertly showed me a "thumbs up" sign.

"Seems to me," I said, "that sooner or later we will be up-linking changes to the vehicle and eventually this will be routine. Who here has a technical, not emotional, reason to NOT do this?" Crickets…

"Do it!" Meeting adjourned. It worked and the next day we were ready to take the first picture of earth.

Earlier in the program I argued against doing precision alignments and measurements. These alignments measure the relation of the sightline of the telescope with the attitude reference system, primarily the star trackers. This allows one to know precisely where the telescope is pointing. My rationale was that even with the worst manufacturing tolerances we could at least get close to a target and then we could tweak the numbers to hone the precision. Sort of trial and error to get the system calibrated. But, nope, I lost, the analysts insisted we do these complicated and time consuming alignment measurements on the spacecraft while it was still in the factory. It took two days to do these alignments. And, they did them three times!

It was time to take the first picture and someone asked, "What should we take a picture of?" John Neer, the CEO and founder of Space Imaging, said, "DIRT!" And everyone laughed. (Earlier I suggested Area 51; everyone thought it was a cool idea, but it never happened... well, not right away anyway.)

We looked at the next orbit path and Reno, California, would be just about straight down (nadir) but still within range of the Thornton tracking station. So we got the longitude and latitude for Reno and when the bird came over Alaska we up-linked the commands instructing the vehicle to take its first picture, a picture of Reno, Nevada, when it made contact with the Thornton ground station.

Before it went out of contact at Alaska, the stored program commands were retransmitted by IKONOS and the ground guys verified that all the instructions for the first picture attempt were up-linked properly. It would now be several minutes until contact at Thornton, Colorado, where we were located.

After the several minutes, the large screens lit up and we could see the satellite telemetry being displayed; we had contact with the bird. We watched an animated display that showed an interpretation of the spacecraft orbiting above the earth. This rendition keyed off actual flight telemetry being received "real time," which showed an animated version of the vehicle rotating to take a picture. We "saw" the door that protected the telescope open and we then saw the vehicle scan the earth—just like a Xerox machine. The door closed and it went out of contact a few minutes later.

The data was processed and many people gathered around a monitor to look at the very first IKONOS picture from space.

Chunk, chunk, chunk, chunk; just like that, the picture formed on the screen. We could see roads, mountains, buildings, trees. A tremendous cheer exploded from all! We did it! We had what John Neer called, "First light."

The cheers died down and the screen operator manipulated the picture with the mouse and someone said, "Dat ain't Reno!"

"So what are we looking at?"

"Beats me."

Jim VanPernis said, "Wait, I was in Reno a few weeks ago, I'll go get my Reno map from the car."

He came back in what seemed like five seconds; I think he was so excited he ran through the walls. He opened the map and after a few moments he said, "Hey, this isn't Reno."

"Yeah, look, here are the railroad tracks, I-80, and that bend in that road, right there."

"You're right! We just took a picture of Sparks, Nevada!"

They got the latitude/longitude and calculated that we were off by 0.5 degrees. So we ended up changing the flight software to compensate. The next pictures were right on target. So much for doing alignments.

The next day John Neer passed out miniature flashlights with "First Light" written on them. John was so very thrilled with the results of our efforts and for successfully accomplishing his vision, as were we. John was the one that had pushed this program from the beginning. His persistence with the government bureaucrats and Lockheed management enabled the world to have satellite imagery. John did that. We all saw the first light and we were beyond joy.

A few more days passed and Space Imaging (SI) started taking hundreds of images; the number grew and grew. We still had many on-orbit tests to do to "sell off" the spacecraft to SI.

After being in Thornton two weeks I decided to go home. I booked a flight for Friday about 5:30 p.m. so I would have to leave around 3:00.

It was 2:30 and the guy in charge of the ground equipment told me to go outside and watch the very large dish antenna track the satellite during the next contact, in ten minutes.

"Hey, good idea."

I walked through the building and made my way out the back door, across the parking lot, and I walked up to a concrete pad on which was mounted a very large antenna; it was mounted on an equally large pedestal. This antenna "tracked" the satellite as it came overhead, so this would be fun to watch.

It was pointed at the horizon like a snoozing dog waiting for a car to chase. I looked at my watch; two minutes until contact. The 17,500 mph satellite was streaking across the North Pole and Canada making its way to Colorado. With the IKONOS satellite orbiting at 620km (~400 miles) when it came over the horizon at Thornton it was directly overhead in northern Canada.

One minute. I expected the antenna to smoothly start tilting upward as it would come closer.

Thirty seconds. The red warning light mounted on a pole next to the antenna came on; standard procedure.

Then WHAM! The entire antenna jolted so hard and so loud I back peddled almost falling backward on my tush.

Then another WHAM...WHAM...WHAM. Then thunk-a, thunk-a, thunk-a, thunk-a. On each thunk-a the antenna tilted about half of a degree. Thunk-a, thunk-a. Cables rattled back and forth. I saw the joint between the pedestal and the concrete pad get larger, then smaller, then larger, then smaller at each thunk-a; it wasn't much, but I could see it was moving!

Five minutes into the ten-minute pass, thunk-a, thunk-a, thunk-a! I backed away. The dish was straight up, like a bowl on a table. It started to rotate down the other side; that would be towards me!

I'm outta here, I said to myself, and I went back into the control room.

The ground equipment guy was standing at the control room door like a proud father, "So what do you think of our antenna?"

"Well...frankly it's pretty scary!

"Scary?"

"Well, yeah; it goes thunk-a, thunk-a. I thought it would go hmmmmm. The whole thing shakes. And what a wallop when it made first contact; scared the crap outta me. Now I know why you guys have the red light out there."

Two heads popped around the door jamb; one head said, "Yeah, it does that in 'auto track.'"

"It wasn't in auto track," the other head said.

"Oh yeah," I added, "I'm not sure, but the pedestal kinda rocks. I'm no ground guy but I'd say it's not bolted down so well. But, hey, what do I know?"

The ground guy's eyes were the size of parabolic antennas!

Swwwishhhh! They were gone.

I left for the airport and the next morning I got a call at home from one of my guys onsite.

"Bill, are you sitting down?"

"Yeeeees…what gives?"

"They went out and inspected the antenna. The dish pivot bolts were gone; gravity was holding it in the 'saddle,' and, get this, you know how the pedestal was supposed to be bolted to the concrete pad with a circle of bolts? Well, half of the circle had no bolts; the other half were loose. Holy shit! And the media is going to be here Monday for the public revealing of the first (calibrated) image! Of Washington, D.C., no less!"

"Can they fix it?"

"Well, there's a crew coming right now with a crane to pull the dish off. It'll be tight."

Sunday, 9:00 p.m.; fixed.

The press came Monday. I was there; I flew back Sunday night and was a bystander to all of the Space Imaging mucky-mucks hobnobbing with the press as they proudly revealed the first high resolution commercial image from space—and rightly so.

Now the antenna goes "Hmmmmmmmmmmm."

175

36

The **IKONOS spacecraft required** some minor tweaking but that's all. It's been on orbit now for nearly twelve years and was only designed for seven. It was the most rewarding program in my career.

After several months of proposals to Space Imaging, Inc., for possible follow-on spacecraft that never came about and probably never would, I decided to accept a job as the spacecraft manager for a program that was to use the IKONOS bus; the mission and payload were different. It was small and fun, for a while.

With all of the new mission requirements, it turned out that the only thing reminiscent of the IKONOS bus was a magnetometer; everything else had changed, so it was basically a new spacecraft. And we got power on this new spacecraft in twenty months, which, I think, was a Lockheed Martin record.

Dad passed away from congestive heart failure. At his funeral I spoke of his always saying to me, "You're a freshman all over again." And I said the same to him; he was a freshman all over again wherever he might be.

A few months later, I was notified that I was to be honored with an award for leading the team that got the early power-on of our new spacecraft. It was to be held in Washington, D.C., all expenses paid, and Joyce could come too. Tom Dougherty, the program manager of this program at the time, nominated me.

This award was the pinnacle, recognition-wise. And I certainly give Lockheed Martin credit for this recognition (or at least for going along with Tom's recommendation). I knew this was really the symbolic end but I didn't mind because I felt that I had reached my aerospace goal;

six years before, I was an IKONOS console guy. Sure I could go on; I could have pushed for a director's position, but it was souring even with the recognition of this award, and I didn't want to turn into some bitter old curmudgeon.

I rented a tux and Joyce and I flew to D.C. We took a taxi to a really nice hotel, then spent the next day walking around the Mall. We saw the White House and the Capitol. A taxi took us back to the hotel where we got dressed up in our evening garb. Joyce normally didn't like company events like the annual Christmas parties but this was different. I could feel her support and her joy and I knew she wanted to do this for me.

The awards ceremony was held in the National Air and Space Museum where they had reserved it for what seemed like several hundred Lockheed Martin people. It just so happened that we were one of the first in line for photos with the CEO.

CEO Bob Stevens (L) with author and wife, Joyce
at NOVA award ceremony; October 22, 2004
Courtesy of James Tkatch

Joyce and I walked around the museum before the dinner. We saw the real X-15, my science project subject from many years before, and we looked at other aircraft and displays. We got some distance between us, as sometimes happens when we roam festivals and museums at different paces. Suddenly Joyce back-tracked and called me over to a display that she'd found. As I entered the display area I immediately saw a rather nice exhibit of space shuttle wind tunnel models. They had a few of the actual stainless steel models in a case as well as some photographs. Most I was familiar with. Then I saw a photo of one of my Orbiter Aerodynamic Heating test models; it was the model that created the ice that crashed into the rear of the wind tunnel at Ames, and it was in the National Air and Space Museum! Suddenly I felt the time difference; not between San Jose, California, and Washington, D.C., but from 1973 to 2004.

I was elated seeing the wind tunnel photos and models, and I thought of my many trips to Manchester, Tennessee. I felt the progress I had made since then, not only professionally but as a person. I was grateful for my experiences and I was proud of my accomplishments over those years. Few knew, or could know, all that I had done, but that didn't matter.

We all filed into the museum IMAX Theater for the award ceremony. There were just a few speeches, very nice speeches by the way, and then the awards were announced for various categories such as patents, teams, technical achievement, and leadership.

I was to be presented with one of the highest awards in the company: The Lockheed Martin NOVA Award for Leadership "For leading the team to an early power-on of a spacecraft program."

As I stood in line with other award recipients waiting to go on stage to shake the hand of Mr. Bob Stevens, CEO of Lockheed Martin, I pictured events throughout my life that brought me to this event: Mother pointing out the B-29 bomber photo in the department store, the models on my pegboard, my first model rocket flight, the science projects, Mother and Dad beaming during my college graduation, Dad watching Joyce and I drive off to California, the shuttle wind tunnel tests, the ramjet tests, saying, "Spacecraft is GO!" for the IKONOS launch, and finally mentoring "the kids" on these last programs.

I remembered when I was a kid viewing the photograph of an F-84 in the Air Force road show trailer, and then viewing the first commercial high-resolution image of the earth from our IKONOS satellite.

I moved up in line; I could see the stage and the packed audience. I knew that Dad was beaming once again. I couldn't see him, but he was there. And Mother was in Texas ecstatic over my success. I could feel Joyce's glow as I stepped onto the stage. I had done it. I had reached the top of the Mike Mars ladder.

Author (right) accepting NOVA award for leadership from Lockheed Martin CEO Bob Stevens; October 2004

Epilogue

The new program did, however, take a toll on me. I was working very long hours for three years and the stress level was exceptionally high. My mother died about six months after my NOVA award and I started to think about early retirement. I just couldn't bear the stress anymore. My body was telling me that daily. I resigned as space segment manager and transferred to the Military Space line of business. It was a much lower stress job, which helped me transition to retirement and free-lance consulting.

I certainly have no regrets about my thirty four years in the aerospace industry. I was never laid off and I am fortunate enough to say that I reached my goals. Although I never excelled in the corporate executive ranks, rising to space segment manager on a few programs and program manager of IKONOS was fine with me. I had more fun getting it done.

I enjoyed what I did and I certainly took the work seriously, but to some, I may have seemed a bit too cavalier and "unprofessional" by having a sense of humor at work. There will always be serious issues and serious times and sincerity is appropriate then, but most of the time there is room for laughter. It doesn't mean one is not committed; rather, it reflects the joy of the work. Humor can build cooperative relationships between people, and *that* is critical to the success of any project.

I decided to leave early, at fifty-seven, to perhaps begin something new. It became clear to me that my methods, intuitiveness, and other traits were not fitting into the new process-oriented methods of operations and management. And while I certainly appreciate my career and Lockheed Martin, I was becoming the dinosaur, even though I still hold firmly to my methods and philosophies taught to me by early

Lockheed senior engineers and management. What I learned from them may not meet the current industry standards but we got satellites built, tested, and launched successfully.

In April of 2007 Joyce and I retired to southern Appalachia—the Blue Ridge Mountains of Hendersonville, North Carolina. We enjoy the mountains and the mild four seasons.

Just before we left for North Carolina, John Neer, a VP at Lockheed Martin in Denver (the ex-Space Imaging executive that gave us the "first light" flashlights and *the* founder of IKONOS), saw me privately on my last day at Lockheed Martin; he presented me with a photo of himself with Arthur C. Clarke, along with a handwritten note. Arthur C. Clarke was quite interested in commercial imaging and had befriended John years earlier.

John told me something that day that I'll never forget. He said, "You are one of a few people who led the program that literally changed the world. No one will ever know our names or what we did but *we* will know. IKONOS was the first high-resolution commercial imaging satellite. Look at all the imagery on Google and Yahoo today. We started that."

Those words echo in my mind.

I currently do part-time consulting, and perhaps in a few years I can sit and enjoy retired life full-time...and fish.

Made in the USA
Middletown, DE
07 December 2018